T0318492

The Hunger Games

The 2012 film *The Hunger Games* and its three sequels, appearing quickly over the following three years, represent one of the most successful examples of the contemporary popularity of youth-oriented speculative film and television series. This book considers "The Hunger Games" as an intertextual field centred on this blockbuster film franchise but also encompassing the successful novels that preceded them and the merchandised imagery and the critical and fan discourse that surrounds them. It explores the place of *The Hunger Games* in the history of youth-oriented cinema; in the history of speculative fiction centred on adolescents; in a network of continually evolving and tightly connected popular genres; and in the popular history of changing ideas about girlhood from which a successful action hero like Katniss Everdeen could emerge.

Catherine Driscoll is Professor of Gender and Cultural Studies at the University of Sydney. Her research focuses on youth and girl culture, popular culture, modernity, and rural cultural studies. She is also author of *Girls, Modernist Cultural Studies, Teen Film*, and *The Australian Country Girl*.

Alexandra Heatwole is a researcher in media and gender studies, specialising in girl studies, youth culture, speculative fictions, and sexuality and reproductive technology. Since her doctorate, *Renegotiating the Heroine: Postfeminism on the Speculative Screen* (Sydney, 2015), she has published on princess culture and girl heroes.

Cinema and Youth Cultures

Series Editors: Siân Lincoln & Yannis Tzioumakis

Cinema and Youth Cultures engages with well-known youth films from American cinema as well the cinemas of other countries. Using a variety of methodological and critical approaches the series volumes provide informed accounts of how young people have been represented in film, while also exploring the ways in which young people engage with films made for and about them. In doing this, the Cinema and Youth Cultures series contributes to important and longstanding debates about youth cultures, how these are mobilised and articulated in influential film texts and the impact that these texts have had on popular culture at large.

Clueless
Lesley K. Speed

Grease
Barbara Jane Brickman

Boyhood
Timothy Shary

Easy A
Betty Kaklamanidou

The Hunger Games
Catherine Driscoll and Alexandra Heatwole

L'Auberge Espagnole
Ben McCann

For more information about this series, please visit: www.routledge.com/ Cinema-and-Youth-Cultures/book-series/CYC

The Hunger Games
Spectacle, Risk and the Girl Action Hero

Catherine Driscoll and Alexandra Heatwole

Frontispiece, Poster for *The Hunger Games: Mockingjay Part 2*

Routledge
Taylor & Francis Group

LONDON AND NEW YORK

First published 2018 by Routledge

2 Park Square, Milton Park, Abingdon, Oxon, OX14 4RN
605 Third Avenue, New York, NY 10017

Routledge is an imprint of the Taylor & Francis Group, an informa business

First issued in paperback 2020

Copyright © 2018 Catherine Driscoll and Alexandra Heatwole

The right of Catherine Driscoll and Alexandra Heatwole to be
identified as authors of this work has been asserted by them in
accordance with sections 77 and 78 of the Copyright, Designs and
Patents Act 1988.

All rights reserved. No part of this book may be reprinted or reproduced or
utilised in any form or by any electronic, mechanical, or other means, now
known or hereafter invented, including photocopying and recording, or in
any information storage or retrieval system, without permission in writing
from the publishers.

Notice:
Product or corporate names may be trademarks or registered trademarks,
and are used only for identification and explanation without intent to
infringe.

British Library Cataloguing-in-Publication Data
A catalogue record for this book is available from the British Library

Library of Congress Cataloging-in-Publication Data
A catalog record for this book has been requested

ISBN: 978-1-138-68306-8 (hbk)
ISBN: 978-0-367-73452-7 (pbk)

Typeset in Times New Roman
by Apex CoVantage, LLC

**For Ruth,
and for Norma and Jim**

Contents

List of figures   viii
Series editors' introduction   ix
Acknowledgements   xi

Introduction: 'The Hunger Games'   1

1 Choose your own adventure: survival, adulthood,
   and other fantasies   19

2 Katniss Everdeen, girl hero   35

3 Team Katniss: in the arena of romance   51

4 The train from District 12: Panem as dystopia   68

5 'The Hunger Memes': film, fans, and speculation
   as critique   85

Bibliography   99
Index   107

Figures

Frontispiece, Poster for *The Hunger Games: Mockingjay Part 2*   iii
0.1 'The Katniss Barbie'. © Mattel   5
0.2 The 74th Reaping of District 12, *Film 1*   11
1.1 Surveillance map of Panem, *Film 2*   30
1.2 Katniss, pre-Games Flickerman interview, *Film 1*   32
2.1 Snow's granddaughter with her family, *Film 3*   40
2.2 Katniss as action hero, *Film 2*   45
3.1 Katniss, Peeta, and family, *Film 4*   52
3.2 Mockingjay 'propos' production, *Film 3*   62
4.1 President Snow's surveillance, *Film 2*   72
4.2 Katniss looking into an arena camera, *Film 1*   73
5.1 The Hunger Games Exhibit (Sydney, December 2016)   89

Series editors' introduction

Despite the high visibility of youth films in the global media marketplace, especially since the 1980s when Conglomerate Hollywood realised that such films were not only strong box-office performers but also the starting point for ancillary sales in other media markets as well as for franchise building, academic studies that focused specifically on such films were slow to materialise. Arguably the most important factor behind academia's reluctance to engage with youth films was a (then) widespread perception within the Film and Media Studies communities that such films held little cultural value and significance, and therefore were not worthy of serious scholarly research and examination. Just like the young subjects they represented, whose interests and cultural practices have been routinely deemed transitional and transitory, so were the films that represented them perceived as fleeting and easily digestible, destined to be forgotten quickly, as soon as the next youth film arrived in cinema screens a week later.

Under these circumstances, and despite a small number of pioneering studies in the 1980s and early 1990s, the field of 'youth film studies' did not really start blossoming and attracting significant scholarly attention until the 2000s and in combination with similar developments in cognate areas such as 'girl studies'. However, because of the paucity of material in the previous decades, the majority of these new studies in the 2000s focused primarily on charting the field and therefore steered clear of long, in-depth examinations of youth films or was exemplified by edited collections that chose particular films to highlight certain issues to the detriment of others. In other words, despite providing often wonderfully rich accounts of youth cultures as these have been captured by key films, these studies could not have possibly dedicate sufficient space to engage with more than just a few key aspects of youth films.

In more recent (post-2010) years, a number of academic studies started delimiting their focus and therefore providing more space for in-depth examinations of key types of youth films, such as slasher films and biker films, or examining youth films in particular historical periods. From that point on, it was a matter of time for the first publications that focused exclusively on key youth films from a number of perspectives to appear (*Mamma Mia! The Movie, Twilight* and *Dirty Dancing* are among the first films to receive this treatment). Conceived primarily as edited collections, these studies provided a multifaceted analysis of these films, focusing on such issues as the politics of representing youth, the stylistic and narrative choices that characterise these films, and the extent to which they are representative of a youth cinema, the ways these films address their audiences, the ways youth audiences engage with these films, the films' industrial location, and other relevant issues.

It is within this increasingly maturing and expanding academic environment that the **Cinema and Youth Cultures** volumes arrive, aiming to consolidate existing knowledge, provide new perspectives, apply innovative methodological approaches, offer sustained and in-depth analyses of key films, and therefore become the 'go to' resource for students and scholars interested in theoretically informed, authoritative accounts of youth cultures in film. As editors, we have tried to be as inclusive as possible in our selection of key examples of youth films by commissioning volumes on films that span the history of cinema, including the silent film era; that portray contemporary youth cultures as well as ones associated with particular historical periods; that represent examples of mainstream and independent cinema; that originate in American cinema and the cinemas of other nations; that attracted significant critical attention and commercial success during their initial release; and that were 'rediscovered' after an unpromising initial critical reception. Together these volumes are going to advance youth film studies while also being able to offer extremely detailed examinations of films that are now considered significant contributions to cinema and our cultural life more broadly.

We hope readers will enjoy the series.

Siân Lincoln and Yannis Tzioumakis
Cinema and Youth Cultures Series Editors

Acknowledgements

The foundations of our argument here were sketched in our essay, 'Glass and Game: The Speculative Girl Hero', published in *New Directions in Popular Fiction* (Gelder 2016). We also draw on Alexandra's doctoral thesis – *Renegotiating the Heroine: Postfeminism on the Speculative Screen* (2015) – and on some of Catherine's earlier work, including *Girls* (2002) and *Teen Film* (2011).

We want to first acknowledge the Department of Gender and Cultural Studies at the University of Sydney, an environment that has helped shape our work. This book is also indebted to the efforts of Yannis Tzioumakis and Siân Lincoln, editors of this series on youth and cinema. Yannis and Siân set out to build a cohort of scholars interested in youth on screen around the world, and their achievement has helped us all. We also want to thank Ken Gelder, for his editorial work on the rambling draft of an essay that always wanted to be a book, Deborah Heatwole, who assisted with proof-reading, and our colleagues in the International Girls Studies Association who have helped create a scholarly space for approaching girl culture with the multi-disciplinary seriousness it demands.

We also have some more personal thanks to offer. Catherine: Thanks, as always, to my family and friends for continual support, especially Sean Fuller and Dawn Moore, who shared more of these movies with me than they could have wanted. For my part, however, this book is dedicated to Ruth Talbot-Stokes – beloved sister, faithful ally, and fellow fantasy fan. Alexandra: Thanks particularly to Deborah and Sam Heatwole for their support, both practical and otherwise, and for giving me the books in the first place. Thanks also to Amanda Cuthbert and Gabriel Gilbert for being my fellow film watchers, and to Megan, and Lucy and Charlotte, two generations of girls on fire. For my part, this book is dedicated to my grandparents, Norma and Jim Fairfield, whose imagination and storytelling inspired a lifelong love of all things fantastic.

Introduction
'The Hunger Games'

This book explores the Hunger Games films, produced by Lionsgate between 2012 and 2015. One of the most successful recent youth-directed film franchises, the series consists of: *The Hunger Games* (Ross 2012, from now on *Film 1*), *The Hunger Games: Catching Fire* (Lawrence 2013, *Film 2*), *The Hunger Games: Mockingjay Part 1* (Lawrence and Ross 2014, *Film 3*), and *The Hunger Games: Mockingjay Part 2* (Lawrence 2015, *Film 4*). We will consider a range of approaches to these films across the following chapters, but centrally as a spectacular hybridization of teen, action, and science fiction film which, in their contemporary media environment, we argue could only have a girl hero. Drawing on the films, Suzanne Collins's Hunger Games novels (2008–2010) on which they are based, and the merchandising and fan practices to which they are tied, we situate these films as a crescendo in a long trajectory of representing girl heroes on screen. We will emphasise how these films draw on recent developments in representing gendered youth on film and television, as well as on the distinctly cinematic tone and pacing of Collins's novels, and link the franchise to a 1990s turn in popular discourse on girlhood often associated with the slogan 'girl power'. This orientation towards changing images of and discourses on girls is central to how the Hunger Games films function as 'youth cinema'.

The impact of family and gender on young lives, the limits and significance of agency within the highly institutionalised monitoring of youth, the meaning of immaturity and adolescence, and the association of youth with social continuity and cultural change are all important to these films. Moreover, the Hunger Games narrative requires that these themes are framed as political questions and staged through a story about rebellion against an oppressive state. This book thus does not centrally deal with the Hunger Games films from an aesthetic point of view. Instead, we are interested in taking these films, and the broader franchise they now dominate, as a collective text for discussing how twenty-first century cinema imagines youth, and especially girls. We will particularly focus on the franchise's hero, Katniss Everdeen: as a spectacle of power, vulnerability, resilience, and transformation; as an icon of virtue, reward and promise; but also, paradoxically, as a figure for the risks attendant on the complex significance of girlhood today. There are, of course, other characters in the Hunger Games story, and other narratives in play than the ones centred on what Katniss can and cannot do, and at what price. But Katniss dominates all elements of the franchise, and that dominance is crucial to understanding its success at this point in the cinematic history of representing youth.

We will also use the Hunger Games films to explore how cinematic stories about youth interact with other aspects of the contemporary media environment. The following chapters not only emphasise the adaptation processes that situate the Hunger Games films in 'intertextual' relations to the Collins novels. They also take the Hunger Games as a 'transmedia' object, incorporating the fields of promotion, commentary, and critical and fan reception that surround the films. Just as importantly, however, we want to give historical context to the ideas about youth, girlhood, genre and narrative from which the Hunger Games films emerge, and approach the films using textual and theoretical analysis with due attention to the cultural historical moment they represent. The rest of this chapter introduces some key themes and critical tools that weave through our analysis in the following five chapters.

Franchising girlhood: from first-person narration to the Katniss Barbies

The Collins novel trilogy, *The Hunger Games* (2008, *Book 1*), *Catching Fire* (2009, *Book 2*) and *Mockingjay* (2010, *Book 3*), are the obvious starting point for any discussion of the Hunger Games, and Katniss's centrality to these is clear. Each novel is narrated from her first-person point of view, *Book 1* opening as follows: 'When I wake up, the other side of the bed is cold.' (2008: 3) What Katniss perceives and knows largely limits our reading experience, so that we must gradually accumulate what this opening means across the first paragraph: that the cold is noticeable because that other side should be occupied by someone called Prim, from whom 'I' seek warmth, but who has bad dreams and might seek comfort elsewhere. We quickly learn that Prim is the narrator's younger sister, but other details need to be more actively gleaned from Katniss's narration, including how their shared bed of 'rough canvas' signifies the family's poverty. This narrative style means the reader only gradually comes to doubt whether Katniss knows all we might want to know. She is also what literary critics call an 'unreliable narrator': sometimes clearly mistaken and very often unsure of events she cannot see or the motivations of others.[1] Yet she is already the moral compass of the story before this becomes clear. The books never invite us to doubt Katniss's intentions, or whether she should triumph, but gradually important limits on her knowledge and understanding do invite doubts about how completely she *will* triumph.

The films build on this identification with Katniss, substituting the 'I' of Katniss's narration with the camera's identification using both her visible responses and her visual perspective. Although they also contain original material allowing the viewer to see and know things Katniss does not, including all the behind-the-scenes elements of 'The Hunger Games' as a television text within the text (from now on The Games), this informs how we look through and at Katniss rather than qualifying her centrality. As theorists of the 'cinematic gaze' have long argued, film as a rule relies on character identification (far more commonly than first-person narration is used in literary texts), and so the equivalent opening scene of the movie does more than tie us to Katniss's point of view.

Film 1 opens with a series of prologue screens and establishing shots that build a picture of Katniss's world: the nation of 'Panem' (all that remains of Earth, as far as we know) and, more specifically, Katniss's home in 'District 12'. The prologue text establishes the facts of Panem's post-war treaty, which requires the annual 'Reaping' of teenagers (one boy and one girl chosen by lottery from each of twelve districts) for a nationally televised fight to the death. The accompanying shots juxtapose the polished media framing of The Games as television broadcast and the poor rural setting in which we meet our protagonist. The first shot of Katniss (Jennifer Lawrence) is not of her waking but of her comforting Prim (Willow Shields), whose fear at her first Reaping, now she has turned 12, underscores the necessity of resisting this brutal ritual even as it indicates Katniss may be the one to help. The simple styling of the Everdeen sisters and their home contrasts starkly with the ornate styling of the media commentators, just as the nursery song Katniss sings to soothe Prim counters the public callousness of their discussing the political necessity of The Games. Although both *Book 1* and *Film 1* take time to confirm that Katniss will be the hero such a situation demands, the film conveys far more certainty that the audience should identify with Katniss, using lighting, framing, and editing to keep Katniss's presence visible in shots and sequences ostensibly focused on other characters. Although she will still soon have enough evident flaws to be an interesting character, the film rapidly identifies with Katniss's strength and virtue, inviting a different set of audience and fan dynamics. It expands the franchiseable potential of Katniss, and at the same time opens up space for alternative readings focused on characters or stories marginalised by this dominance.

Our focus on the Hunger Games franchise is not a matter of stressing its popularity. In a franchise, the named object is duplicated, elaborated, and repurposed across media, multiplying not only instances but meanings and opportunities for attachment. Discussing the Hunger Games as a franchise stresses the inseparability of the different components it unites, including lateral ties between the four films but also connections across different media. The success of the film adaptations starring Jennifer Lawrence as Katniss, grossing nearly US$1.5 billion in North American theatrical box-office revenue alone, and similarly successful in many other countries,[2] fed back into sales of Collins's novels, the expanding fandom for which provided dedicated repeat film viewers. This is clear from online fansites and in the promotional covers added to re-issues of the books, featuring iconography from the films' promotions. Somewhat paradoxically, this iconography consists chiefly of symbols generated to sell Katniss as rebel figurehead in propaganda recruiting for a war against the dictatorship of President Coriolanus Snow and the indiscriminate consumption of life in the Capitol (Panem's capital). Using this iconography to sell myriad Hunger Games objects, from school stationery to makeup lines, has an at least ambivalent meaning for audiences familiar with the story.

The range of 'Katniss Barbie' dolls (Figure 0.1) is exemplary. The three available dolls, designed with reference to Katniss's style in the films, throw into sharp relief the internal story about marketing Katniss and highlight the importance given to Katniss's various 'looks' in the films compared to the books. For example, the Katniss Barbie wears her hair in a single over-the-shoulder braid. This is a signature Katniss style in the films, identified as her authentic at-home look and emphasised as essentially Katniss by various forms of appreciation. When he thinks he will die, her love interest Peeta (Josh Hutcherson) lifts and caresses this braid, and fans in the Capitol are seen to wear their hair this way to identify themselves with Katniss. Just as importantly, fan identification with or cultural commentary on Katniss's character uses this braid as a succinct way of signifying Katniss that is only minimally supported by the books.

Although such transmedia strategies as those linking the films, the fans, and the Katniss Barbies are by no means confined to youth-centred narratives, they are common in marketing to the young. The concept 'transmedia' was first coined by Marsha Kinder (1991) to discuss the relation between advertising and popular media texts' address to children, stressing how their interest moved fluidly across different fields of consumption. Kinder's account of transmedia objects positions them as a form of 'intertextuality', citing Mikhail Bakhtin's argument that meaning is always 'understood against the background of other concrete utterances on the same theme . . . made up of contradictory opinions, points of view and value judgments' (1991: 2 quoting Bakhtin). For Kinder, this is principally a way of understanding how audiences operate – how, for example, children might understand the

Figure 0.1 'The Katniss Barbie'
© Mattel

relations between a television programme and advertising juxtaposed with it. Her ideas influenced the more famous work of Henry Jenkins and other writers discussing how audiences *participate* in the production of meaning. Across Jenkins's work, this participation has been understood in different ways, but consistently draws on theories insisting that the meaning of popular culture can never be fully determined by authors/producers.[3] We also accept this premise, with reference to the shifting relations between: different elements of the Hunger Games franchise, how different citations and tropes become visible to different audiences, and relations between the franchise and its possible – at times, contradictory – interpretations.

Roland Barthes' theory of intertextuality, which posits that any text is 'a tissue of quotations drawn from the innumerable centres of culture' (1977: 146), is not only a theory of textuality but also, as John Frow suggests, of how genres work (2014: 45–50). We are also interested in genre as a way of understanding how audiences make meaning of the Hunger Games, and as a way of understanding how the Hunger Games films work as adaptations. Intertextuality describes a field of connections between texts, but genre helps explain how some such connections become dominant guides for interpretation. Any individual textual component can invoke generic associations that transform the meaning of other components (see Altman 1984). These generic attachments may be simultaneously about narrative content, visual style, and audience relations, and the Hunger Games' guiding generic associations are not only to science fiction/fantasy, romance, action, horror, and teen/youth film genres, but extend to literature, television, video games, and music video. They also draw on genres which do not ostensibly take cinematic form – most importantly, reality television and fanfiction.

The impact of genre on the Hunger Games is not only a matter of identifying groups of texts the films resemble or invoke. The word 'genre' slips from that kind of categorization into an opposition between film more broadly and 'genre film', a label identifying some kinds of film as more predictably tied to known plots, styles, and modes of address. The Hunger Games films are also 'genre films' in this sense, aligned with film genres that more visibly deploy their conventions. This alignment with formulaic popular culture is furthered by their having at their centre a beautiful girl. The association between girls and commodity culture has a long history and the conjunction of generic conventionality, visible fan culture, and prolific merchandising all accentuated this association for the Hunger Games films.

This brings us to two influential critical templates which have underwritten much scholarly and popular discussion of the Hunger Games films (although often only implicitly in the case of popular discourse). Each will return in different forms across the following chapters. The first is a Marxist critical framework which emphasises the association between modern girlhood and capitalist commodity culture, centred on the use of girl images to sell to every marketing demographic. While this book cannot be a theory primer, we will attempt to adequately contextualise our critical tools; and to consider the working of commodity culture, both in Panem and the worlds of its audiences, one must start with 'commodity fetishism'. This concept was coined by Karl Marx, in 1867, to describe the way commodities are detached from the complex industrial and social relations that produce them, leaving them almost magical objects of 'worship' (Marx 1976). In the later work of Theodor Adorno and Max Horkheimer, this analytic shifted to focus on media as the primary object of consumption. Their model of media consumption positioned girl fans of popular movies and music as exemplifying the false promises and inauthentic pleasures of mass culture (2002: 97). And in 1967, Guy Debord used commodity fetishism as the basis for his Situationist *Society of the Spectacle*, arguing that modern media-saturated social relations were detached from sociopolitical structures and also human interest.

We will consider how Debord's spectacle applies to The Games themselves, and Katniss's navigation of them, but the Situationists also argued that a girl ideal is crucial to this alienated society. This was phrased superlatively by the collective Tiqqun's *Raw Materials for a Theory of the Young-Girl* (1999; see Driscoll 2013), which can be summarised by the following quotations: 'The YoungGirl is the place where the commodity and the human coexist in an *apparently* non-contradictory manner' (17); and 'The YoungGirl occupies the central kernel of the present system of desires' (9). Drawing on Debord, Tiqqun identify the problem of commodity fetishism, and capitalism itself (24), with what they see as girls' own efforts to become commodities. Given that girls have thus long been viewed as the 'model citizen' of 'commodity society' (Tiqqun 2012: 4), and that both commodity society and model citizens are oppressive forces and enemies in the Hunger Games story, there are necessarily contradictory forces energising the girl image in this franchise.

This overlaps with the second critical template we want to introduce here: the long history of passionate feminist debate about the objectification of girls and women. The Hunger Games films belong to the context of these debates in the second decade of the twenty-first century, when commodification has long been not only something decried by feminists but also a tool used to express feminist ideas. Across the following chapters we will situate the Hunger Games in a feminist history too easily simplified by a 'waves' model that pits 'second wave' critique of the traps of girlish pleasures against 'third wave' demands for access to all pleasures, and a 'fourth wave' still tentatively entering this debate through both individual and collective forms of media celebrity. In locating the Hunger Games franchise in this historical *situation* (a word we choose advisedly), we want to consider both this story's emphatic critique of the reduction of people to images and the role of image and imagination in possibilities for positive change. The Hunger Games films offer possibilities for identification with multiple versions of Katniss, and the objectified iconic versions cannot be separated from the critical ones even while they remain incompatible. Katniss is not simply a female type, of the kind Virginia Woolf stressed women writers would not produce (1945: 95–100), and she is not reducible to the impossible ideals Betty Friedan saw as tormenting women and distracting girls from more specific life-goals (2001: 126–135). She also cannot be reduced to the erotically dissected object of the cinematic gaze analysed by Laura Mulvey in the 1970s, operating both as the central agent of action and perception on screen and the primary screen object 'to-be-looked-at' (1975: 11). Moreover, Katniss is highly conscious of her double role as agent and object, and her story is partly about the different forms that role can take, making the Hunger Games films particularly interesting for feminist analysis.

'Keeping the horror fresh and immediate': speculative adolescence on screen

Fantastic stories in which a girl saves a universe that both is and is not ours are now very numerous. They appear not only in literary and cinematic texts, but on television, and in comics and video games, among other examples. This figure of a singularly special girl clearly appeals to millions, but she is also clearly distinguished from a real world (if only by the spectacular powers she fights). Perhaps she: leads a team safeguarding the universe against evil overbalancing good (Sailor Moon in Naoko Takeuchi's Sailor Moon franchise, beginning with a 1991–1997 manga); leads defence of the human world against continual attempts to overrun it from dark other-worlds (Joss Whedon's Buffy the Vampire Slayer franchise, beginning with a 1992 film); is pivotal to preventing the rise of an evil wizard-lord (Hermione Granger in the Harry Potter franchise, beginning with J.K. Rowling's 1997–2007 books); galvanises defence against a tyrannical new government (Tris in the Divergent franchise, beginning with Veronica Roth's 2011–2013 books); or re-frames the interstellar struggle against tyranny as a girl as much as a boy story (Rey and Jyn in the 2016 and 2017 iterations of the Star Wars franchise, beginning with George Lucas's 1977 film). Other speculative franchises feature girl screen heroes and many more discrete films or series could be listed, but the increasing visibility is undeniable.

We call the figure that unites these increasingly popular stories since the 1990s, 'the speculative girl hero' (Driscoll and Heatwole 2016). If fantasy and science fiction books seem to have led the way in reimagining girl heroes in this period, they were always importantly influenced by new screen images of the girl who fights, or at least fights back, and film and television have in turn taken up and extended this literary shift. Film and television adaptations of older fantastic stories now highlight girls in more heroic roles: reorienting the girl roles for films based on C.S. Lewis's Narnia (2005–2010); expanding (Arwen) and adding (Morwen) youthful-appearing female roles in the Peter Jackson Tolkien films (2001–2014); or fleshing out the girlhood of Wonder Woman for Patty Jenkins' 2017 film reboot. It may seem, in the present dominance of super-heroic action films, that there are few equivalent female-centred screen images, with 'super-heroines' appearing as off-siders (Batgirl through to the Black Widow) or secondary villains (early Catwoman or Poison Ivy). The minor exceptions, *Catwoman* (Pitof, 2004) and *Elektra* (Rob Bowman, 2005) – both injured women fighting back against a world that failed to protect them – are dwarfed by the success of *Wonder Woman*, a 'golden age' superhero (Klock 2002) supported in her world-encompassing virtue by a newly full girlhood story. But the apparent singularity of *Wonder Woman* requires some qualification.

First, despite several film series about the boy superhero Spider-Man since the 1990s, the other heroes of the Marvel and DC studio blockbuster wave are not boys in the sense that the previous lists feature girls. Youth has been more important to recent super-heroic screen narratives on television, where series like *Smallville* (WB/CW, 2001–2011) and *The Flash* (CBS, 2014–ongoing) sit alongside girl-centred stories like *Supergirl* (CBS/CW, 2015–ongoing) and *Crazyhead* (E4, 2016–ongoing), as well as alongside more ensemble narratives, like *Misfits* (E4 2009–2013) and *DC's Legends of Tomorrow* (CW, 2016–ongoing). Speculative television more generally tends to feature adolescent and younger adult characters, as in *Supernatural* (WB/CW 2005–ongoing), *Being Human* (BBC3 2008–2013), *The Vampire Diaries* (CW 2009–2017), and *Teen-Wolf* (MTV 2011–ongoing); although, as with *Buffy* (WB/UPN 1997–2003), longer series eventually qualify their youth-centred narratives. This is partly because television is more easily consumed in domestic spaces and often without special access requirements. Television and books have thus together furthered demand for cinematic girl heroes like Katniss.

The broad characteristics of this speculative girl hero should also be sketched here. She is fundamentally brave and honest, with courage extending both to intrepid physical action, even when she fights reluctantly, and to critique of the way the world works around her, although she is often less insightful about herself. She thus opposes the traditional representation of girls as prizes rather than agents in myths, legends, and folktales. She also always represents the challenges posed by expected gender roles, as well as the comforts and pleasures they can offer. She often positions these contradictions as unresolvably complex, with the sacrifice of some pleasures or forms of self-validation required to choose others. Our interest in this girl hero arose from the way that, despite her strengths, this girl thus seems open to feminist critique because her action and achievement are often accompanied by images of femininity.

Of course, girl heroism is not the only aspect of the Hunger Games films worth discussing in a book about their representation of youth. Katniss herself does not exhaust the significance of youth to imagining a new future for Panem, and an overview of the roles played by age in the franchise will be helpful here. There are, broadly, four types of individuated characters, and the symbolic importance of youth crucially defines them all. The first (small) group consists of Katniss's sexualised love interests: Peeta and Gale (Liam Hemsworth). These strongly differentiated characters do more than flesh out Katniss's character by way of her options, drawing on highly recognisable teen romance conventions. They also stand for social difference in District 12, and different sociopolitical choices, and their youth means Katniss must try and ascertain not only who they are but who they are becoming in terrible circumstances. Like all youthful characters in this story, their suffering seems more tragically serious because of other experiences foreclosed on, and in this respect, not only Peeta but also Gale is a tribute to The Games, indicating its destructive impact.

The second (largest) group of characters consists of the Hunger Games competitors. There are twenty-two tributes, other than Peeta and Katniss, in the 74th Hunger Games (*Film/Book 1*) – all adolescents aged between 12 and 18 selected as ideal for television spectacle as well as for political suppression because they are young. The most prominent are Rue (Amandla Stenberg) – the youngest, whom Katniss takes as a sister-substitute and tries to save, then mourns – and Cato (Alexander Ludwig) – the final antagonist who represents everything villainous that childhood training for The Games can produce. There are not strictly any 'tributes' in *Book/Film 2* because the 75th Games are a special 'Quarter Quell', with past Games 'victors' reaped again. There are once again twenty-two competitors, beyond Peeta and Katniss, this time of various ages. The five significant characters include the elderly Mags (Lynne Cohen), and two middle-aged victors, Beetee (Jeffrey Wright) and Wiress (Amanda Plummer), but the two most important are young adults – Finnick Odair (Sam Claflin) and Johanna Mason (Jena Malone). This range finally proves Katniss's authority to represent Panem, rather than merely the symbolic power of sacrificing youth. Perhaps in part because they know they are at risk as part of a plan to end Katniss's popular influence, and certainly because many are conspirators in a plot to save her and spark a revolution, all the competitors focus their attention on Katniss – either as the one they must defeat or the one they must save. Of those who survive, only Beetee is not youthful, and in *Book 3/Films 3–4* he is quickly incorporated into the social structure of District 13 while Johanna and Finnick remain important indices of the damage done by The Games, even to winners.

The third group – the first we meet as they help convey what kind of girl Katniss is – are her family and neighbours, the 'people' of District 12. In the films, neither the mayor nor 'peacekeepers' are characterised, so these residents represent the downtrodden ordinary life of Panem. Only three are important, with recurring characters from the novels like Gale's family, Greasy Sae from the black market, or Madge the mayor's daughter, reduced or merged to throw these few into sharper relief. Haymitch Abernathy (Woody Harrelson) needs separate consideration later, as his mobility between District 12 and the rest of Panem sets him apart, leaving only Katniss's sister and mother. Her mother (Paula Malcomson) seems largely helpless in *Film 1*, and does not even have a given name. Although given a minor healing role in the later films, she mainly functions to show why Katniss has developed superior self-reliance. This is dramatised further by Prim. As the only other individuated adolescent in District 12, and the first whose name we see called for Reaping, only for Katniss to volunteer in her place, Prim first stands for vulnerability (Figure 0.2). She demonstrates Katniss's capacity to nurture and empathise when her other attitudes and actions might seem harsh. In the later films, Prim becomes more independent, but this only heightens the tragic impact on Katniss when her sister is killed during the war. As heralded by Rue's fate, Prim only just seems to begin growing into whatever would have been herself when Panem kills her.

The final group unites Katniss's adult supporters and enemies who together form the social field that Katniss must struggle to defeat, save, and renew. They are principally the results of what is wrong with Panem. As the previous rebellion ended with The Games treaty seventy-four years before *Book/Film 1*, even President Snow (Donald Sutherland) and the rebel president Alma Coin (Julianne Moore) grew up under its influence – Snow being 75 and Coin around 50 when first introduced. Snow is evil

Figure 0.2 The 74th Reaping of District 12, *Film 1*

the way The Games are cruel, and it is thus fitting that his whole life is coextensive with them. He also represents Panem's failure to nurture anything of value, symbolised by his undying/un-aging white roses – an image of artifice unmarked by experience. Most characters, however, like Plutarch Heavensbee (Phillip Seymour Hoffman) and Coin, represent more complex versions of the harm done by self-interested exploitation of others. The audience is invited to share Katniss's uncertainty about their motivations and likely actions, and to reconsider them as Katniss does. The most fully characterised is Haymitch, who is also the hardest to place in our taxonomy. He is a surviving victor-tribute, although never in the arena during the films; he is one of the District 12 constituents Katniss represents; and he works variously as Katniss's antagonist and supporter, often positioned as having a special understanding of her weaknesses and potential. The novels specify that Haymitch won the 50-year Quarter Quell, and is thus somewhere between 37 and 53, but he continues to represent the sacrifice of youth imposed by The Games. Having spent twenty-four years training the children of his district for death, Haymitch is routinely drunk, and his eventual role in Katniss's survival and the rebel victory never changes this. Haymitch is never quite redeemed, but also never quite at fault. In many respects he is Snow's opposite – a critical guide who knows and represents the failings of Panem but cannot change them directly.

Although Katniss survives the eventual showdown with both presidents, and they do not, it is never entirely clear that she is victorious, or what she has won. In this respect, Katniss's story resembles many youth film dramas in which the achievement of a more mature understanding of the world is a very ambivalent victory. Katniss's increasing maturity is tracked by her changing relations to others, including her love interests, as the conventions of youth cinema would expect, but also to the world of adults defined by their occupations whom Katniss must either oppose or rely on for survival and, later, achievement of her changing goals. Most effective emotional and practical support is offered by the stylist Cinna (Lenny Kravitz); and the irony of a stylist being the only entirely trustworthy and reliable adult is an important one. Although the overall narrative is highly ambivalent about their work, professionals in image production are among Katniss's most reliable supporters. These include the public relations representative Effie Trinket (Elizabeth Banks), and Katniss's makeup team in the first two films and her film production crew in the final two films. That the dramatic conflict propelling the overall narrative is centrally about image production becomes clearer when we notice that her most important adult antagonists are also focused on image control. In addition to the two presidents, there are the two Gamemakers, Seneca Crane (Wes Bentley) for the 74th Games and Heavensbee for the 75th, and the television host Caesar Flickerman (Stanley Tucci). Compared to these image-workers, there is far less agency among the peacekeepers and soldiers who are occasionally distinguished by particular events. Though their responses may range from oblivious brutality to self-sacrificing sympathy, they generally follow the orders of politicians. Politics and the media are represented as violent forms of cooperating image manipulation that the military merely reinforces. They constitute concrete regimes of oppression against which better stories/images are a necessary, and perhaps the most effective, response.

Youth at risk: imagining heroes for a (neo)liberal state

The importance of youth to fantasy and science fiction is continuous with the importance of youth to social analysis, which takes youth as an index of the present and sign of the coming future. To conclude our introduction, we turn to some dominant ideas about the social context in which the speculative girl hero emerged. Just as youth cinema is not exclusively Anglophone (Shary and Seibel 2007; Driscoll 2011: 149–162), the social and cultural theories that surround this girl hero's renovation since the 1990s have an international frame of reference. They are, however, principally produced in, and principally refer to, societies dominated by transnational commodity capitalism and its tensions with forms of national state welfare. This section introduces a series of concepts that seek to understand this context, and which help us understand the world imagined by the Hunger Games. We will briefly introduce the Foucauldian concepts of disciplinary power, governmentality, and neoliberalism, then discuss postfeminism, and finally turn to the concept of risk society.

Collins has repeatedly said that her Hunger Games novels are 'basically an updated version of the Roman gladiator games', and that she was inspired to write it while

> channel surfing between reality TV programs and actual war coverage. On one channel, there's a group of young people competing for I don't even know; and on the next, there's a group of young people fighting in an actual war. I was really tired, and the lines between these stories started to blur in a very unsettling way.
>
> (Collins, quoted in Margolis 2008)

In drawing on this contemporary media collage to tell her story about bread and circuses (Panem being named after the Latin word for bread and The Games operating as its circus), Collins produces a sharp historical contradiction that adds frisson to the story. And the figure of young people competing for media supremacy offers a powerful interpretation of the contemporary world.

Across a number of publications, Michel Foucault argues that modern social power shifted away from the direct display of a sovereign's right to kill. In 'Society Must Be Defended', Foucault states:

> I wouldn't say exactly sovereignty's old right – to take life or let live – was replaced, but it came to be complemented by a new right which does not erase the old right but which does penetrate it, permeate it. This is the right, or rather precisely the opposite right. It is the power to 'make' live and 'let' die.
>
> (1997: 241)

Foucault called these new technologies for assessing and managing populations 'biopower'. The operation of state power was supplemented by the management of people, which he also refers to as 'disciplinary' power. While the iconic Foucauldian account of disciplinary power is the self-monitoring of prisoners who are institutionally compelled to fear they might be being watched at any time (1977: 202–203), in *The History of Sexuality* he clarifies that this shift to disciplinary power encompasses new modes of education and parenting, as well as new ideas about the sexed self (1978: 104). Given these historical shifts, the capital punishment aspect of The Games that makes Panem seem so archaic is made 'almost believable' (Todorov 2000) for the twenty-first century by media technologies that tie it to contemporary anxieties. Panem works through a mesh of sovereign and disciplinary power – through schools as well as gladiatorial combat, through the state-media complex and biopower as well as through floggings, torture, and war.

These modern modes of government centre on the birth of 'liberalism', the philosophy of democratic government grounded in a social contract between free-acting individuals and the state embodied in civil institutions. In his analysis of liberalism, Foucault also coined the term 'governmentality' to discuss how states developed mechanisms for 'the conduct of conduct' (Gordon 1991: 2) that require, encourage, and reward the self-government of individuals through laterally dispersed operations of governance. These lead to his accounts of 'neoliberalism', a now very widely used term – in popular as well as academic contexts – to describe the integration of these governmental operations with free market economics. The concept of neoliberalism has been progressively detached from economic theory and is now used to describe Western society in general. As Wendy Brown exemplarily puts this argument, in 'neoliberal society' 'everything is "economized" and . . . human beings become market actors and nothing but, every field of activity is seen as a market' (Brown 2015).

The concept of 'postfeminism' now operates as an account of what neoliberalism means for, and does with, the achievements of feminism (although it too once meant something far more specific). In its popularisation since the 1990s, it has become closely linked to images of successful girlhood – what is sometimes called 'girl power' feminism and which Anita Harris discusses as the rise of iconic 'can-do girls' (2004a). Can-do girls, appearing in a variety of popular media sold predominantly to girls and women, are more imagery than reality – they are a girl spectacle in Debord's sense. As Harris argues,

> What is not highlighted, but is fundamentally important here, is that material resources and cultural capital of the already privileged are required to set a young woman on the can do trajectory. Instead, the good or bad families, neighbourhoods, and attitudes are held to account.
> (Harris 2004a: 35)

The contemporary girl-powered girl faces an equally contemporary potential for failure, making girlhood a subjectivity in need of special concern and protection. It matters in this sense that speculative girl heroes belong to worlds in which many recognisable contemporary obstacles to girlhood success have been removed. For example, the importance of class is often demobilised (the Hunger Games is interestingly an exception), often by loosely feudal social orders in the case of fantasy or by technocracy in the case of science fiction; and while central characters are often unmarked by race (implicitly white), the possibilities of an imaginary world can obscure this for both creators and audiences.

While invocations of girl power now seem intrinsic to post-1990s preteen and adolescent girl culture, this emerged simultaneously from girls' activism – the slogan itself belonging to post-punk musicians and zinemakers in the United States (US) in the early 1990s – and from a media-driven moral panic with the girl at its centre. The 'riot grrrl' origins of girl power have over time been dwarfed by less confrontational versions of popular music and publishing for girls, most famously the Spice Girls in the United Kingdom (UK) later that decade. But girl power also took its force from campaigns stressing girls' capacities among parents and institutions, inspiring new popular texts and lobbying for new girl-centred policies, although these clearly supported the interests and presumed the opportunities of some girls more than others. These campaigns can be summarised using Mary Pipher's influential popular psychology text, *Reviving Ophelia*, which famously referred to girls entering adolescence in the era after 'second wave' feminism as 'saplings in a hurricane' (1994: 22). This hurricane was driven both by the resilience of traditional images of ideal girlhood and by the choices made available to them by feminist success in the areas of non-reproductive sex, careers for women, and life narratives independent of marriage and family. The burden and costs of fulfilling the hope created by those successes generated what later theorists refer to as a self-destructive 'melancholia' (McRobbie 2009: 111–119) in response to a 'postfeminist sensibility' pervading media culture (Gill 2007).

In the realm of speculative fiction, the risks heroines face are often concrete and immediate – death, injury, social or even world-destruction – but less tangible risks associated with postfeminist girlhood are also evident. Beyond staying alive and saving others, Katniss and other contemporary 'young adult' (YA) heroines remain anxious about how they should appear and relate to others in often very traditional ways. Hegemonic expectations for gender performance are important in many of these narratives, but in the Hunger Games, resistance to them could mean death. Katniss's survival is linked to her ability to represent a desirable and desiring subjectivity. She is called upon to be both special and a manageable citizen in some fundamentally girl-oriented ways as well as to fight savagely for her own survival while proving her individual worth by generosity towards others. In particular, she must learn to embody a femininity articulated through fashionable style that she finds baffling and pointless in ways that echo much of McRobbie's argument about a 'postfeminist masquerade' that encourages girls' complicity in hegemonic gender codes (2009: 59–72). Performance of this masquerade is required even while its superficiality is stressed, and as the typical goals of a *bildungsroman* must be subverted in favour of survival.[4]

What 'can-do' girls can do is achieve successful womanhood, and because of the impossible vagueness this involves and the immanent risk of failure, this goal is framed as a process of risk management. Thus, the postfeminist story of girl empowerment aligns with neoliberalism in that successful life outcomes are determined by detecting and avoiding risks and managing opportunities by making the right personal choices. Such individualisation downplays structural and cultural inequities, including in presuming that gender itself is no longer an obstacle given past feminist successes. Evaluating Katniss's choices by any of these standards is, however, largely rendered meaningless by the fact that youth in Panem do not face similar struggles to produce a viable adulthood, and our presumptions about girlhood risks are made strange when thrust upon Katniss. Except for those born in the Capitol, and we know very little of youth there, who one will be is largely a foregone conclusion. When chosen as tribute Katniss is hurled from a world relatively unconcerned about youthful identities to one where construction of such an identity is necessary for survival. Her identity is suddenly mediated by the values of the Capitol, where 'sponsors' can decide whether she lives or dies and management of one's self-image is a principle concern. Only on television, that is, does Katniss become a hyperbolic parable of contemporary girlhood.

The promotion slogan for The Games is 'May the odds be ever in your favor', but we first hear this phrase used sarcastically in a conversation between Katniss and Gale, which makes clear how well the people of the districts know the odds are stacked against them all. There is always a good chance of being chosen in the Reaping, especially for the more disadvantaged who will trade extra inclusions of their name in the lottery for food tokens called 'tesserae'. There is little chance of winning those Games, especially for those already undernourished. And there is no chance of living a life not dominated by continually weighing the risk of starvation against the fear of being apprehended for violation of trade, labour, hunting, and myriad other rules and the risk of the tesserae. This brings us to the concept of 'risk society', another interpretation of neoliberalism which at first glance is also tied to a society very different from Panem. Risk society is also discussed as 'reflexive modernity' in order to argue that it is organised around the 'hazards and insecurities' produced by modernity itself (Beck 1992: 21), from environmental degradation to systemic poverty. Here it matters that Panem is not just a fictional world, but an imagination of the US in the future, after an environmental disaster that flooded the land, reshaping society. The risks and insecurities underpinning life in Panem are meant to be both like and unlike our own, including in situating youth as the pre-eminent image of our future-oriented social anxieties at both personal and world-shaping levels.

In a 2008 review of *Book 1*, novelist Stephen King declared that 'Reading The Hunger Games is as addictive (and as violently simple) as playing one of those shoot-it-if-it-moves videogames in the lobby of the local eightplex; you know it's not real, but you keep plugging in quarters' (King 2008). He felt Katniss was too conveniently spared actual harm, need, or horror, but also that the books hinged on whether or not you cared about what happened to her, and he did. However, once *Film 1* had become a blockbuster hit, in 2013, King revised his opinion, saying he 'didn't feel an urge to go on' with the story. While reserving his more detailed disdain for the Twilight and Fifty Shades franchises, King now grouped them all as obviously stories for girls because nothing was really at risk in them (King, quoted in Stedman 2013). King's own stories specialise in encounters between innocence and monstrosity, but in this case he is looking for the wrong kinds of harm and risk. There are no killer clowns hiding in sewers in the Hunger Games, but there is an oppressive web of institutional and individual limits that make youthful engagement with the future feel impossible. It is Katniss's confrontation with, and transformation of, this system that makes her not simply heroic, but a *girl hero*.

Notes

1 More precisely, Katniss is what William Riggin (1981) calls 'the naif' type of unreliable narrator, for which her youth aids style as well as characterisation.
2 The worldwide box-office taking is estimated at around US$3 billion – see, for example, boxofficemojo.com.
3 As well as Bakhtin and Barthes, such influences on Jenkins include Michel De Certeau, Janice Radway, John Fiske and Constance Penley. Although relevant to our argument, we will not be able to discuss these further.
4 A bildungsroman is a story of becoming oneself, coined in 1819 by Karl Morgenstern.

1 Choose your own adventure

Survival, adulthood, and other fantasies

The Hunger Games films draw on many genres, but not always in the same way. Although we argue that all their generic engagements converge on the importance of youth, the genre with which we need to begin is speculative fiction, an umbrella term used to unite stories that imagine another world across many media. In advertisements and in their opening sequences, the most immediately apparent feature of these films, before any action takes place, before any question of character is raised, is that they are set in a world that is not ours. This chapter takes up three approaches to the importance of fantasy in the Hunger Games. Our first section establishes a critical history for talking about fantastic fiction, and its relevance to the Hunger Games, while the second begins with the role youth plays in speculative genres before turning to how this appears in the Hunger Games. These are necessary critical foundations for all the following analysis, including in the last section of this chapter, which acknowledges that the Hunger Games franchise also draws on very different popular fantasy genres by turning to its commentary on and use of reality television.

The attractions of genre

Between the two dominant forms of speculative genre the Hunger Games is clearly more science fiction than 'high fantasy', because it invents a future for the world its audience is presumed to share, and because it diverges from that world by technological rather than magical means. The key difference between technology and magic in this sense is that the former is concretely imaginable. Thus, in a world that has rockets and planes, interstellar travel is more readily conceivable and the possibility of alien civilisations is raised. In a world that routinely uses microchips and all scales of camera for surveillance, virtual reality and digital connectivity for gaming, and digital special effects for film, television, and video, the technologies represented in the Hunger Games can be imagined, even if we cannot currently create all the traps featured in The Games or used for defence of the Capitol. Every strange element of Panem — full body skin tints, rosters of daily tasks encoded on forearms, or controlled herds of hybrid killer monkeys – are extensions of technologies that already exist. This is key to the story the Hunger Games tells about youth, and the fact that science fiction is a form of fantasy is crucial in this respect.

We thus want to take a step back to some canonical theories of fantastic genre. In Tzvetan Todorov's famous 2000 definition, the phrase 'I nearly reached the point of believing' is 'the formula which sums up the spirit of the fantastic' (2000: 18). Fantasy represents what might be felt as believable, although it is not true. The much-discussed changes to Disney princesses over time exemplifies what this means in the field of girl culture (Hains 2014; Heatwole 2016). Disney's 2015 version of *Cinderella* is no less fantastic than its 1950 iteration, but the earlier story would now fail the test of a girl audience's expected pleasures and desires, and could never be almost believable. One thing that has changed for that audience is an expectation of girl heroism that even the corporate imprimatur of Disney cannot over-ride. Highly successful films like *Brave* (Andrews and Chapman 2012), *Frozen* (Chris Buck and Jennifer Lee 2013), and *Maleficent* (Robert Stromberg 2014), featuring multiple examples of female heroism, sketch this broad expectation (Heatwole 2016: 6–7). Today, even Sleeping Beauty (in the case of *Maleficent*) must actively choose her path and interrogate the workings of her world.

Todorov offers us a usefully subtle framework for this, noticing that 'Either total faith or total incredulity would lead us beyond the fantastic: it is hesitation which sustains its life' (1970: 18). This hesitation can be between real and unreal, between 'natural' and 'supernatural' (19), or between known and unknown technologies. Speculative genres seek to imagine new parameters for social experience that feel as yet undefined, and what Todorov calls the 'reader's hesitation' (18–19) expresses the necessarily dialogic relation between an imagined world and the world from which it is read. Speculative genre requires the audience enter a world organised by a visibly different set of rules, but also never leave behind awareness of that difference.

The Hunger Games is also, however, heroic fantasy, and characterising Katniss's individual bravery and resilience and the justice of her cause is aided by aligning her with a very familiar structure for such stories. In narrative theory focused on the 'heroic quest', we can see how an intertextual field of inference adds significance to Katniss's every move, adding to her decisions the weight of redefining the world. From the most famous theories of how myths, legends, folktales, and popular speculative genre work, we will mainly reference Joseph Campbell (1949) and Northrop Frye (2004), who both also discuss the quest hero as paradigmatically adolescent.

In *The Hero With a Thousand Faces*, Campbell argues that 'The standard path of the mythological adventure of the hero is a magnification of the formula represented in the rites of passage: separation – initiation – return: which might be named the nuclear unit of the monomyth' (1949: 30). The youthfulness of a hero on this journey emphasises a passage to being someone special – even unique. They often begin the story suffering from clear disadvantage or need, emphasising the problems in the world at hand. Even more often, however, they come from unknown or concealed origins, emphasising the scarcity of skills needed for the task at hand, which often includes youthful energy and passion. As Frye explains, 'The enemy is associated with winter, darkness, confusion, sterility, moribund life, and old age, and the hero with spring, dawn, order, fertility, vigour, and youth' (2004: 110). All these points are true of the Hunger Games, and the story quickly establishes, by such generic cues, that Katniss will be the hero Panem needs, although exactly how this will be manifested is never certain until the end.

Frye refers to heroic quest narrative as the 'romantic cycle', and the foundational such cycle as the sun-god's renewal (110), which is why heroes travel 'perilously through a dark labyrinthine underworld full of monsters between sunset and sunrise' (112). While the end of this cycle is always a return (in the classical sense of 'a romance'), bringing the hero back to an ordinary world, now free to live in it, this comes about through a transformative crisis. Campbell calls it 'a supreme ordeal' and 'expansion of consciousness and therewith of being' (1949: 246), while Frye refers to it as *sparagmos*, 'or tearing to pieces', which precedes 'the reappearance and recognition of the hero' (2004: 113–114). Each book/film in the Hunger Games franchise, and the story overall, fulfils this pattern, with the crucial exception of Katniss being a girl. Frye draws on comparative mythology to represent this cycle as structurally requiring a male actor, who leads change while the female is aligned with reproduction and continuity. This hero is distinguished from women, as Campbell says more specifically, because 'woman is life; the hero its knower and master' (1949: 101).

That this overlaps with Laura Mulvey's account of the 'male gaze' as the locus of seeing and knowing in narrative cinema (1975: 12–13) points to a dominant popular cultural theme, and raises again the question of change. Many scholars have questioned the relevance of Mulvey's model beyond a particular moment in the history of distinguishing mainstream Hollywood and art cinema, and arguments about the cinematic working of a 'female gaze' have also been proposed, although these generally agree there is a stark on-screen opposition between gendered bodies and looks (e.g. Taylor 2014). The problem with formalist theories, whether Frye's or Mulvey's, is not that they are old-fashioned, or too formulaic, as evidenced by the ease with which the Hunger Games fits the heroic formula. It is that they are necessarily insensitive to history. Contemporary speculative girl heroes offer something more than a girl in a boy's role, as we will consider again in the next chapter with closer reference to action film. While girl heroes are now common, they typically use the familiar boy-hero formula to articulate a difference which does not erase the pressures of that expectation.

A range of feminist critics have intervened in the heroic 'monomyth' to emphasise the consistency of its relegation of girls and women to the role of prize/victim. Teresa de Lauretis' essay 'Desire in Narrative', which first appeared in 1984, emphasises that both Frye and Campbell were indebted to Sigmund Freud, and defines 'narrative form', after Jurij Lotman, as 'a passage, a transformation predicated on the figure of a hero, a mythical subject' (1984: 113). De Lauretis also, however, connects this to the patterns, tropes, and topoi of 1980s cinema, where 'narrative itself takes over' from this 'function of the mythical subject' (121). In all, she notices the importance of an opposition between 'mobile' characters – agents 'who can change their place' in the imagined world – and 'immobile characters or personified obstacles . . . standing for (on) a boundary which the hero alone can cross' (118). In the popular cyclical structure of heroic narrative, she argues, an 'endlessly repeatable' story appears – one of 'entry' and 'emergence' relative to a feminised 'plot-space' (ibid.). This hero must be male because this plot-space is 'not susceptible to transformation' (119) – to life, death, history, and narrative.

The value of de Lauretis for us is her focus on questions of change, asking how these earlier formalist approaches are continued rather than presuming the model is eternal. Speculative genres change continually. Brian Attebery, in 2004, distinguishes contemporary fantasy from 'traditional myth' by its 'dependence' on pre-existing stories – its drive to 'be understood' by 'channeling the fantastic imagination through . . . psychological and social codes' (301). Insofar as fantasy perversely depends on mimesis (296) – on being recognisable as well as being inventive – it often works with 'iconic' imagery. As Attebery suggests, these images are 'concrete emblems of problematic or valuable psychological and social phenomena' (299) through which audiences are invited to recognise a familiar lexicon, heightening the sense that these genres afford special 'insight' into their social world (ibid.).

As a tool for prising meaning out of Katniss's story, the heroic romance formula is best understood as generating iconic meaning. A passing allusion can activate this whole set of expectations, and continue to do so even if contradicted by other story elements – and Katniss's story does much more than allude. For example, entering The Games arena involves walking onto a spectacularly visible stage rather than entering an underworld, but it still functions as a heroic trial in *Books/Films 1–2*, no less than the literal undergrounds of *Book 3/Films 3–4*. Similarly, although Katniss is not destroyed as she becomes the Mockingjay, a symbolic association between the Mockingjay and the phoenix remains apparent in the novels, the films, and the iconography circulating in the broader franchise. At the same time, however, Katniss's version of the phoenix is tinged with Cinderella images of a makeover transformation, and this indicates a rather different aspect of the story.

Novelist Ursula K. Le Guin also argues that the fantasy genre, while a game 'played for the game's sake' at one level, is also 'a game played for very high stakes' (1979: 145). It works, she thinks, much like a dream (in what she understands to be Freud's sense), and demands 'a different approach to reality, an alternative technique for apprehending and coping with existence' (ibid.). In her essay 'From Elfland to Poughkeepsie', Le Guin discusses the kind of representation that makes fantasy work, focusing on internal consistency – anything is possible in speculative fiction as long as it rings true for the imagined world. Extolling this inventiveness, Le Guin defines fantasy by 'the creator's voice' and against the 'comfortable matrix of the commonplace' (154), which is a 'substitute for the imagination' allowing only 'ready-made emotional response' (155). We suggest, however, that the familiar is also important in fantasy; offering what makes it *almost* believable. A panorama of expected responses and presumed desires are involved in anyone understanding a 'creator's voice'. In the Hunger Games this includes, for example, expectations that girls are self-conscious about their appearance, allowing only a slight reference to any girl's reflection on how she looks to work as characterisation. Allusions to both generic and real-world expectations tie the Hunger Games' Mockingjay-phoenix to makeover narratives in a contradictory girl-image which is *both* commonplace and iconic.

Tribute children

It remains worth asking why the heroes of speculative fiction are so often young. Why are girls and boys, or young men and women, so often at the forefront of defence against imagined evil forces? One possible answer would cite the presumed audience for these stories, but if Hunger Games novels seem to clearly be marketed using the YA category the same audience association does not carry directly into films. There, YA stories might be converted into 'family' films (as in the Harry Potter franchise), remain predominantly oriented towards a youth audience (as in the Twilight franchise), or like the Hunger Games films be adapted to action spectacle or some other generic mix with a crossover audience. Moreover, while the

YA category aptly describes a mode of marketing that places books relative to others; it does not predict an audience in the same way as do preschool books. A family audience of parents who read to or with children was crucial to Harry Potter book sales, for example, and an older adult female audience (sometimes labelled 'Twilight Moms') was just as important to the success of the Twilight novels.

The assumption that fantasy literature appeals primarily to adolescents is nevertheless historically entrenched, in the same way it is assumed that video games are played primarily by adolescent boys despite industry reports demonstrating most players are adults and around half are female since at least 2001 (see, for example, Entertainment Software Association 2017). The fans of literary fantasy have always been multi-generational, but at least since the new wave of fantasy literature that appeared following the ground-breaking success of J.R.R. Tolkien's *The Lord of the Rings* (1954–1955), it has been associated with young audiences.[1] This is partly because this new fandom, like video games, was associated with changing times (although with 'new age' sympathies rather than new technologies), but also because a taste for fantasy is associated with escapist incapacity to face reality and thus with immaturity (see Walters 2011). While the youth of the heroes of *The Lord of the Rings* is highly debatable, despite Frodo's impulsiveness being linked to his only just 'coming of age' (or turning 33) at the beginning of the first book (Tolkien 1954: 8), the youthful associations of being a fantasy fan are not. By the early 1950s, popular science fiction too was widely considered to have a dubious influence on young minds, and to have juvenile characteristics (Johnston 2011: 9), especially in the superhero and monster subgenres that are now once again among its most popular forms.

Social anxiety about these forms of entertainment for the young was furthered by 'rite of passage' theories of adolescent social development that also became increasingly popular across the twentieth century. Anthropologists like Arnold van Gennep (1909), Margaret Mead (1928), and Victor Turner (1969), were engaged with the work of psychologists like Freud but also those more concerned with youth culture per se, like Erik Erikson (1968), and they were succeeded by cultural studies and youth studies scholars focused on how youth identities differed from other perspectives on the world. Modern speculative genres have continually been engaged with changing ideas about the importance of youth, and this recognition demands that we think carefully about the role played by youthfulness in the Hunger Games.

At the beginning of *Book/Film 1*, the youth of Panem's districts are all potential tributes for The Games, which memorialise a past war as an ongoing ritual suppression of rebellion. At the government's annual 'Reaping', one boy and one girl (12–18 years) from each district are chosen to fight to the death on television. As this gladiatorial spectacle is compulsory viewing for all citizens, including the families and peers of the tribute children, The Games generalise and individualise the threat extended by the Capitol. Other more banal forms of oppression characterise life in the districts of Panem, including managed scarcity of basic resources to the point where starvation and exposure are common. But The Games as ritual punishment target adolescents to underline the Capitol's power over life and death, leveraging the idea of youth that symbolises the continuation of any family or community. From the moment Katniss is 'harvested' for The Games, what we might call the *state-media complex* suspends Katniss's life between the impoverished mining district where she grew up and a luxurious life in the Capitol. In this state and period of what writers on rites of passage call 'liminality' (e.g. Turner 1969), Katniss might die, might win a victory that saves herself and her family from poverty for life, or might – because from the moment she volunteers for The Games to save her sister Prim she is obviously the hero – change everything. She cannot emerge from this liminal moment the same as she entered.

This is one place to remember Collins's overt references to classical Rome, taken up in various film-script elements, like the staging of gladiatorial training and reference to both 'the arena' and its 'tributes', and reinforced by design elements, including allusions to togas and wreaths in costumes and the use of chariots and amphitheatre seating for parades. While a contemporary audience easily associates an arena with entertainment spectacles, tribute is a far less common term. The figure of tribute children is also a far less comfortable classical allusion than gladiators, despite its broad resonance through well-known mythologies and folktales in which children are given to appease gods or other powers, or to restore an idea of balance. Collins specifies a reference to the legendary Greek hero Theseus, who defeats the Minotaur to end the ritual tribute of fourteen Athenian children (in Margolis 2008), but tribute sacrifices of children are also the stuff of religious scripture and recorded history. In all cases, it is the most extreme of demands.

Modernity extended and specialised longstanding ideas about the special value of children; constituting childhood, as Phillipe Ariès famously argues, as both the pivotal foundation of the self and an icon of innocence (1962: 32 and 100–127). As Joanne Faulkner has detailed (2011), harm to children looms large among contemporary taboos and protecting children has come to commonsensically measure the justice of a society (Grealy 2018). This symbolic significance has been frequently exploited by cinema, and there is a well-established cinematic language for representing the vulnerability of children. The early dramatic sequences of *Film 1* are dominated by building tension through the fearful and anxious faces of increasing numbers of District 12 children as they appear, brushed and washed and neatly dressed in blues and greys and whites, to be subject to the Reaping (Figure 0.2). From the preceding scenes with the Everdeens, we know that every one of those children is accompanied by fearful families who have prepared them for this event, and a focus on Prim builds through cuts to other perspectives as she anxiously takes her place for the first time and is finally chosen for almost certain death.

Prim is presented as a 'little girl', and Katniss's palpable anxiety over her physical and emotional vulnerability is what drives her to volunteer for The Games in Prim's place. It is Katniss's role as Prim's protector, far more than her angry discussion of the injustice of the Reaping with Gale, that positions her as the protector of District 12, and thus Panem. Additional symbolic power is attributed to the girl victim, traditionally presumed to be even weaker than children in general – physically if not also emotionally and intellectually. This is reinforced by the fact that we see more children in District 12 than elsewhere; that in *Film 1* at least we see more children than adults there; and that we also see no other Reaping, except in clips of the moment of announcement. The detailed depiction of Prim's Reaping reinforces the premise that youth cannot be held responsible for the faults of a present society and that sacrificing them at all, and most of all for the sins of the past, is unconscionable.

All the youth of Panem's districts are potential tributes, but not those of the Capitol. This inequity, exacerbated by poorer families having likely taken the tesserae which increases their chances of selection in exchange for extra food, links the Hunger Games to the many stories about adolescent alienation and rebellion that are also stories about social injustice. Youth has many kinds of significance for The Games. The youth of the tributes in *Film 1*, established as a world default, links images of alluring youthful glamour, images of youthful rebellion and violence, and images of unconscionable victimisation.[2] Youth is figured as a fantastic space of trial and revelation and an object of fantastic value, made more complex by the fact that the young must kill as well as be killed and that even the most vicious of those selected remain tributes to the state. The developmental range encompassed by 12–18 plays a role here too, setting trained young fighters against those who still appear to be children.

The emphasis placed on the first Reaping in *Film 1*, and on Prim's age, smallness, and apparently fragility, is also significant. On screens across Panem, the fragility of the youthful body blends with the perceived innocence of young minds to create a spectacle of tragic disruption. Whenever a selected tribute is emphasised as a specially cruel choice, they come from the girl side of the Reaping – beginning with Prim, whose fear acclimatises us to The Games, then equally young Rue, the girl tribute from District 11, whom the books describe as similar to Prim in stature and manner. While in the 75th Games age and infirmity characterise several tributes, the only death we are asked to identify with is the elderly Mags, who volunteered in place of the equally vulnerable Annie (Stef Dawson). No male deaths across The Games call for such focused sympathy. Both an unnamed small boy and Thresh (Dayo Okeniyi) are positioned as tragic deaths in *Film 1*, but the first is a minor character and the second happens off screen.

Rue's elusive smallness is also always emphasised in framing: she appears peering between or from behind things, hiding in small places, or dwarfed by the size of the interviewee's chair. This is punctuated by the grave of songs and small flowers that Katniss makes for her, in a scene of unprecedented tenderness which, anchored by its link to Prim, feels genuine despite being televised, and inspires gifts from Rue's district and mercy from Thresh, its remaining tribute. It also appears to set off the first flickers of public rebellion that grow into a revolution across the story, and is visually and verbally recalled a number of times across the following films: in the shots of Rue's siblings, in Peeta's painting of Rue's grave, and in the shared memory of the scene among rebel commanders in District 13. Prim also reappears as the little girl, although unlike Rue she gets to grow up another year or so. She even shakes off her 'little duck' image to become a battlefront healer, but this only makes her a more moving final innocent victim. Ostensibly killed by Snow's last defence of the Capitol, Katniss and the audience know that Coin (and, in part, Gale) are responsible for the bomb that kills Prim, right in front of Katniss and as the final break with the young Katniss whom we met before The Games.

The girl's greater symbolic weight as a victim is why Gilles Deleuze and Felix Guattari use 'the little girl' to explain the 'haecceity' that marks *becoming* as a mode of subjectivity (1987: 287). Becoming describes the singularity of a subject manifest as a conjunction of forces and actions, rather than being as form. The little girl represents being subject to a multitude of outside influences and investments; becoming herself in passing through them. According to Deleuze and Guattari, the 'body is stolen first from the girl . . . the girl's body is stolen first, in order to impose a history, a pre-history on her' (305). This pre-history is, at least in part, gender, invoking the ways in which regulations and anxieties speak for the girl, objectified by her 'stolen' body. This suggests some useful questions about how the deaths of Prim and Rue are used by various political factions and media producers in the story to propel the narrative of revolution and used by Collins and the films to incite identification. The deliberateness of their spectacular deaths clearly condemns those in power, and yet their use as plot device confirms their effectiveness.

Kerry Mallan and Sharyn Pearce (2003) suggest that young people are particularly saleable images of rebellion in popular media but also the most obviously manipulated by media industries. Mallan and Pearce argue that:

> When removed from any temporal or spatial verities, the commercial representations of youth acknowledge the contradictions in and ambivalence of this stage of maturation and turn angst, rebellion, and even nihilism into desirable commodities. By mapping these psychological conditions specifically onto a young body, the market forces create . . . a site from which ideological or political struggle is elided, reducing the body to a purely superficial or external referent.
>
> (4)

According to this argument, 'youth' itself is commercialised, while the agency of the people 'youth' seems to name is excluded from the image presented. By this argument, young people are interpolated into media texts as voiceless subjects while remaining the media subject of choice. It is thus particularly relevant that the Hunger Games story is directly concerned with whether the individuality of these tribute children, including Katniss, is lost amongst the symbols that represent them. For Anita Harris, it is ironic that young people are meant to express this unrepresented individuality by responding to mass media – by choosing from just such images presented for their consumption. Harris argues that 'Consumption has come to stand in as a sign both of successfully secured social rights and of civic power. It is primarily as consumer citizens that youth are offered a place in contemporary social life' (2004b: 163).

Cue the hunger: reality games

Story formulas in which an adolescent hero is sent to another world often emphasise their fantastic singularity. The hero's specialness can be identified by self-recognition or public acknowledgement, by being 'sorted' (Basu 2013) or chosen. Harry Potter is marked as special when sorted into Gryffindor (but almost Slytherin); Tris is identified as 'Divergent' from all the available factions; and Bella in Twilight is intrinsically desirable to every vampire, although no one initially knows why. Katniss is singled out by her exceptional skill at archery, but 'specialness' in this sense is never just a learned skill but always more innate, and in Katniss's case her survivor attitude is an intrinsic personal quality that encompasses her resistance to the oppressive social order in Panem. Often, these processes of sorting or choosing begin a gradual recognition of the self. For Katniss, however, survival initially depends on building a fiction that hides rather than reveals her own specialness. This fiction presents her as vulnerable rather than heroic, and as reliant on the protective support of her public love interest, Peeta. Paradoxically, however, Katniss's world-changing potential relies on people being able to see her specialness through this fiction – not only Peeta, but all of Panem, who can thus be inspired by her.

Like most young speculative heroes, to reach the point where she will become her future self – the cathartic, world-changing Mockingjay – Katniss must cross the border between a home world and another world where all the meanings and certainties she is accustomed to are transformed. Such transformation can happen through otherworldly avatars, as in Michael Ende's *The Never Ending Story* (1979); by stepping across a literal threshold into another world, as with the Pevensie children in C.S. Lewis's Narnia novels (1950–1956); by discovering a shadow universe co-existing with their own reality, as for Quentin Coldwater in Lev Grossman's *Magicians* novels (2009–2014); or, perhaps most often, by a journey that takes the hero from an ordinary life in which they were relatively unremarkable to one in which they take on greater meaning. These devices can overlap, but it nevertheless is notable that Katniss's journey to the image-world(s) of the Capitol and The Games brings her closer to the commonsense world of the Hunger Games audience rather than further away, as in all the examples we listed above.

The novels make it clear that Panem is built on the post-apocalyptic ruins of the US. District 12 is in the Appalachians (*Book 1*: 41), refracting its history of coal-mining, poverty, and relative cultural marginalisation into the story of Katniss's origins. The Capitol, on the other hand, is in the Rocky Mountains (ibid.) with the other districts located on a partly drowned map of North America that never becomes explicit until the second film (Figure 1.1). But for tethering fantasy to reality, such literal references are not as important as the continuities of media culture, including close reference to the conventions of reality television.

The expanding success of reality television since the late 1990s has diversified the genre's original focus on documenting ordinary lives into a plethora of subgenres in which the central characters may or may not be ordinary, and the lives on screen may be relatively banal or spectacularly manufactured. Indeed, most types of reality television move their on-screen characters along scales from banal to spectacular and from ordinary to special. Susan Murray and Laurie Ouellette identify the following key subgenres: the 'gamedoc', dating, makeover, docusoap, talent contests, court programmes, reality sitcoms, and celebrity and charity variations on most of these (2004: 5). Apart from the court programme, and a case might be made even for that, the framed reality programme within the Hunger Games draws on all these subgenres. While it centrally documents a 'game', that

Figure 1.1 Surveillance map of Panem, *Film 2*

game is about relationships as well as skill, and the central text is framed by accessory programming that makes over the tributes into stars and juxtaposes them with celebrity hosts and commentators who preview each season's contestants and solicit audience identification with their profile.

The Games thus draw on the conventions of 'reality television' in a range of ways that are crucial to the story overall. These include emphasis on a preview of character types from which a live audience helps select the winners of a real-time screened competition; a network of representational skills and their public assessment through a hierarchy of generic cues; and the imposition and editorial framing of risky experiences. Katniss clearly brings special skills to The Games, but there are also aspects of her character that do not work to her advantage in the reality genre, including her reticent blunt persona and her disinterest in gender performance. However, as Haymitch later explains, Katniss's spontaneous courage and sense of justice interrupt the tight generic expectations of The Games as a media package and make her seem spectacularly real. In fact, as much as Katniss is aligned with the generic expectations of specialness that mark a hero, she is aligned with the real-world presumption that conformity to the successful character types of reality television is a moral failure. We should not miss the fact that Katniss's authenticity, which seems so clearly opposed to the conventional types the production emphasises, is clearly visible to the national audience that propels her to stardom. The glimpses of unscripted sincerity that Haymitch lists in *Film 3* make Katniss both a TV star and a political figurehead, and are entirely consistent with the appeal of reality television.

As Murray and Ouellette put it, 'What ties together all the formats of the reality TV genre is their professed abilities to more fully provide viewers an unmediated, voyeuristic, and yet often playful look into what might be called the "entertaining real"' (6). This appeal persists despite the aware-ness, repeatedly acknowledged by the diegetic audience and producers of The Games, that reality television is tightly managed by casting, scripted frames, and narrative editing (5–8). That the audience of The Games loves Katniss, and that the narrative as a whole makes it clear they are right to single her out as worth saving, is thus a clever continuity with the literary device of the unreliable narrator. Although 'much of our engagement with' reality television 'paradoxically hinges on our awareness that what we are watching is constructed and contains "fictional" elements' (7), the viewing pleasure lies in teasing out authentic moments. Like a characterised narrator who is frequently wrong and often confused about what is real, even in her own responses, 'Reality TV promises its audience revelatory insight into the lives of others as it withholds and subverts full access to it' (8).

Book/Film 1 establish that Katniss's greatest weakness is her unwilling-ness to play games of appearances and that one of her core skills is the exposure of lies and false images. But given the paradoxical pleasure of detecting authenticity in the reality genre, her weakness becomes an advan-tage. The books clearly critique many of the workings of reality television, including the conventionality of the stars into which competitors are made over. While the films necessarily mimic the reality genre when they repre-sent it, compromising any clear distinction between commonplace forms of subordinating reality to image, like Katniss's pretty dresses, and the forms that literally manifest state brutality, like the deaths of adolescents trans-formed into memorial images in an artificial sky.

Depersonalising media effects are pivotal to the cruel world order that must be defeated in the Hunger Games. This is what both Katniss and Peeta contest in their attempts to be something other than a screen 'object' and a pawn in the Capitol's games. Always more adept at managing images than Katniss, before the first arena, Peeta says, 'I keep wishing I could think of a way to . . . to show the Capitol they don't own me. That I'm more than just a piece in their Games' (*Book 1*: 71). Katniss gradually comes to understand what he means. As critique of the reduction of people to images is more difficult in film texts that necessarily invites absorption in the screen image, it seems inevitable that the audience is caught up in the pleasures of Kat-niss's transformation from backwoods hunter to television star. Certainly, we walk on stage with Katniss, sutured to her by the camera's look, but this

Figure 1.2 Katniss, pre-Games Flickerman interview, *Film 1*

is an ambivalent moment (see Figure 1.2). While, with her, we are met by rapturous applause and embraced and elevated by a circling camera, the scene is self-consciously overwhelming: the noise of the crowd sonically overwhelms both her and us even as the lights on the stage blind us both. In that moment, neither Katniss nor the audience knows exactly what is happening and must be dragged back to the action by the host/narrator.

The Hunger Games certainly flirts with the pleasures of commodified girl culture, but how exactly it does this is crucial, as we will consider from several perspectives across the following chapters. Katniss's media success story does mirror reality television in the world of its audience, including through unrealistic representations of body image and a strict adherence to traditional gender codes. From a Cinna design that makes her feel like 'a silly girl spinning in a sparkling dress' (*Book 1*: 136) to the 'Remake Room' in District 13 where her team assembles to take her body back to 'Beauty Base Zero' (*Book 3*: 71), Katniss's success is a self-consciously embodied spectacle. But it remains worth considering the films' makeover scenes closely. The first, and far longest, sets an uncomfortable and even unpleasant tone in a coldly blue-lit room like an operating theatre, or a morgue, in which Katniss, dressed in a hospital robe, is whispered over and worked on. Prone on a metal table, framing stresses the limits on what Katniss can see, and dialogue and action indicate that she does not know what they are doing. Later scenes are too brief to maintain these clinical associations, but the simultaneous labour of artifice and erasure of personality successful appearance involves is always stressed. Katniss's celebrity is something done to her, without her willing consent or active contribution.

The use of reality television in the Hunger Games is not confined to such experiences of commodification. However, we never actually look at Katniss in the arena through the lens of a reality television programme. The scenes are not looked at in the way television is filmed. Instead, we are firmly aligned with Katniss's experience rather than a televisual one, so that action is exclusively centred on Katniss rather than edited with cuts away to other contestants. In cinematic terms, Katniss walks on to a reality television set and walks into a film, where she is not just the most popular character but the star. Although differently to the books, then, the films manage to surprise their audience with reminders that a diegetic television audience saw everything they did, without being able to reveal exactly how it was seen. Similarly, while in the books Katniss explicitly worries about whether her actions were always shaped by awareness of the television audience, the films raise this question by jarring juxtaposition of filmic action and its dislocating framing by television hosts, wildly cheering audiences, and other reminders of reception.

Katniss's success in this media environment is enabled by the team around her. Foremost among these is Peeta, who, through a combination of empathetic personality and a less disadvantaged life, better comprehends the media game of winning favour with the audience by manipulations of character and plot. It is Peeta who plays up Katniss's beauty, charisma, and bravery, and who centrally nurtures a love story that will help attract fans and sponsors. However, Katniss's lack of sophistication remains key to the success of this story, from her naïve reactions to Peeta's declarations to her sincere awkwardness in finding herself on stage. Overall, the Hunger Games suggests a confluence of forces is needed to get Katniss through The Games, including the (both real and not real) screen image of the 'The Girl on Fire'. This image is aided by Peeta, Haymitch, and Effie as Katniss's collective public relations team, but most importantly given a name and a look by the stylist/designer Cinna and his assistants. For her interview appearances, Cinna dresses Katniss in uncharacteristically feminine clothing to enhance her on-screen gender identity: sometimes in 'little girl dresses' (*Book 2*: 218) to stress her innocence, and sometimes in smouldering fitted costumes to emphasise her dangerousness. The self-conscious mix of politics and artistry that Cinna represents (even posthumously, in designs he leaves Katniss after his murder in *Book/Film 2*) is most explicit when he is instructed, before the 75th Games, to dress her in a wedding dress the diegetic audience believes she would have worn to marry Peeta. In the films, this dress is more like a Disney princess costume than is the dress of 'heavy white silk' that the books have the audience select in a televised reality competition (*Book 2*: 298). But for both Cinna crafts this white wedding dress to transform into one resembling the black mockingjay birds which have been taken up as a revolutionary symbol after Katniss's first win. In this transformation, which summarises the plot of *Book/Film 2* overall, Cinna's design simultaneously draws on the audience's desire for romantic fulfilment and also names a political struggle which the state-media complex is trying to hide.

Katniss's special abilities are not such skills in representation but rather a combination of physical dexterity, a certain measure of tactical skill (although she often acts instinctively or emotionally), and a refusal to compromise herself. But image politics makes the difference between life and death in The Games. The charisma of Katniss's authenticity is not enough for this, and she needs a support team that expands as her significance does. The later films largely replace the makeover team with Katniss's own film production team (she has both in the books), and the political advisory role is expanded from Haymitch to a team of rebel leaders. With Katniss separated from Peeta in *Film 3* and alienated from him in much of *Film 4*, more personal advice she can trust comes from Prim, or from Finnick. Finnick especially understands the importance of constructing oneself as object (and in a girl-centred text, this un-gendering of sexual objectification is significant).

However, if Katniss's authenticity is not enough to save her life it is still this, more than her courage, determination, or skills as a hunter, that uniquely equips her for heroism in a world of carefully constructed appearances. As Haymitch insists, she is a better political-media-military figurehead when 'unscripted' or left 'alone' 'in the field' (*Book 3*: 89). As the televised action is both real and unreal, Katniss's role as this figurehead is both real and unreal. When *Book 3/Film 4* finally focuses on trying to specify what is true or false about Katniss, through the device of helping Peeta pin down reality after psychological torture, the answers that are 'true' do not exclude the fictions and fantasies that have pervaded her story. The careful construction (and deconstruction) of the unreal, as well as the ways that reality and unreality are blurred, are also important to the ways Katniss is (mis)aligned with the expected narrative of the spectacular girl hero.

Notes

1 For a discussion of the politics of early Tolkien fandom see Glaubman (2018).
2 *Film 2* represents the vulnerability more than the cruelty of The Games competitors, emphasising Mags's physical frailty and signs of physical and psychological impairment among the others. A key visual before the arena has the victors all holding hands to display their unified protest against being selected a second time. A comparatively long shot of the amputated arm of an older man is especially significant given that the movies do not follow the books in representing Peeta and Katniss's physical impairment after the 74th Games (Peeta subsequently had an artificial leg and Katniss reconstructed hearing in one ear). For the filmed story, disability and impairment are confined to older contestants, maintaining the visual equation of youth with expected beauty norms.

2 Katniss Everdeen, girl hero

This chapter offers three different approaches to the kind of girl Katniss Everdeen might be. The phrasing 'might be' is chosen to emphasise the importance of the idea that girls are in a state of *becoming*, whether this is understood in the Deleuzean sense cited in the previous chapter (of continually becoming), or more colloquially as still on a trajectory towards some mature future self. While such assumptions are applied to youth in general, they have been most important to ideas about girlhood, allowing images of girls to effectively invoke contingency and ephemerality (Driscoll 2002). These ideas pervade popular discourse on girls, the cultural forms addressed to them, and the institutions designed to support and guide them. Here we focus on some of the available girl-type stories that inform the Hunger Games films, which are not just sci-fi action films with a romantic sub-narrative that broadens the usual blockbuster audience. They are also films that insert the *girl* idea into every element of that generic hybridity. Here we will consider three approaches to Katniss's girlhood that impact on the films' narrative and visual form: the modern girl, the teenager, and the *girl*ing of the action hero.

Through the looking-glass, and what Katniss found there

In his influential history of the meaning of childhood, Phillipe Ariés makes the following claim: 'it is as if, to every period of [Western] history, there corresponded a privileged age and a particular division of human life: "youth" is the privileged age of the seventeenth century, childhood of the nineteenth, adolescence of the twentieth' (1962: 32). But to the extent that there are fresh meanings given to these ideas during these periods, in forms internationalised by colonialism and global trade and communications, for the twenty-first century it seems clear that childhood, youth, adolescence, *and* 'young adulthood' are complexly tangled together. The earlier meanings have not disappeared, but also converge in a field united by the problem of *maturity*. Debates around identity and development now consider (im)maturity, innocence, independence, and vulnerability together, whether focusing on the sexualisation of children, cultural differences between markers of childhood/adulthood, diverse forms of prolonged adolescent dependence, or proliferating hybrid identity labels like 'tween', 'adultescence', and 'kidult' (for a range of these issues see Crawford 2006; see e.g. Faulkner 2011). In this respect, *The Hunger Games* is a story for its time. The necessity of Katniss taking care of her family while still a young girl and of Peeta rescuing Katniss while still a young boy – but also the incapacity of Katniss's mother, Haymitch, or the voracious self-indulgent consumer-citizens of the Capitol to take greater responsibility for the state of the world – are all elements of this. More generally, while The Games hold children responsible for social stability, these same children are still treated as minors who are not yet citizens.

Ariés's argument about modern ideas about youth centres on seeing in youth the formation of adult character, evident in dialogues that continued through the Western seventeenth and eighteenth centuries. This 'youth' was very specifically male, but it also produced a space for discussing girls, as Jean-Jacques Rousseau's influential 1762 text on the education of the proto-citizen *Emile* and his help-mate Sophie exemplifies (Rousseau 1979). The tensions between a Romantic vision of youthful promise and its guidance by liberal government were widely discussed and necessarily tied to 'the Woman question'. In her 1791 *Vindication of the Rights of Woman* Mary Wollstonecraft famously took Rousseau to task:

> 'Educate women like men,' says Rousseau, 'and the more they resemble our sex the less power will they have over us'. This is the very point I aim at. I do not wish them to have power over men; but over themselves.
>
> (34)

Attention to the self of the girl came to dominate nineteenth-century discourse on childhood. New forms of material culture appeared representing them as girls – advertising, magazines, fashion, and fiction, interweaving with an array of implicitly and explicitly educational texts (see Dyhouse 1981; Nelson and Vallone 1994). New ideas about girls emerged, and the weakness attributed to girls rather than boys took on new dimensions, also linked to a tangle of ideas about seduction and desire which associated innocence, ignorance, and immaturity, but linked these, in modern girls, to curiosity, precocity, and spontaneity.

This emergence of modern girlhood helped fuel and was furthered by the extension of literacy to a wider range of children, available to be addressed as audiences for new communications industries. Although cinema is itself an invention of the nineteenth century, it was not yet the narrative form in which girls became important figures, but new stories and images featuring girls helped shape the movies that followed. The proliferation of popular speculative fiction is also contemporary with this expansion of literacy and of education for girls. Both reframed folktales and new fantastic stories were important among the expanding forms of publishing for children (Zipes 1997), and while girls were not central to early science fiction they were to both these types of fantasy.

Alice's Adventures in Wonderland (2002), the first of Lewis Carroll's 'Alice' books, published in 1865, is often used as a starting point for accounts of children's fiction, and much can still be learned from Alice about fantasy's conjunction with questions about the girl-self. For discussion of girl heroes, for example, it is telling that while Alice falls down a rabbit hole to enter Wonderland, the adventures she has there are not the classical underworld romance we discussed in chapter one. Alice encounters no trial that transforms her. Instead, she encounters a series of vignettes which endlessly question who she is. Finally, she reaches a mock trial with no purpose but itself, and which she leaves in frustration rather than triumph or flight. Alice returns to the known world, then, no more or less expert, heroic, curious, or sure of herself than when she left. The drama of Alice in Wonderland is of her *being* in itself; or rather the unstable problem of who she is.

The opening of the second Alice story suggests why references to her continue to resonate through popular images of girlhood, even if Carroll's original stories are now rarely read by children. In Carroll's 1871 *Through the Looking-Glass*, rather than falling into an underworld, Alice climbs through a mirror into a world populated by her possibilities and impossibilities. This both speaks to the prevalence of narratives, sometimes literally mirror scenes, in which girl protagonists confront who they are and might become, and also invokes a problem. Alice is always *being seen*, and her being seen involves being judged according to expectations about little girls. Any of Alice's temporary transformations pass quickly, returning her to the little girl everyone can see she is (underscored by John Tenniel's illustrations). Speculative girl heroes are often placed in such visualised scenes of judgement, where what they know and do are subordinated to what they look like. Clearly this resonates with Katniss's adventures in her various other- and under-worlds. But it is equally important that when girl protagonists confront such visualization, the scene often inspires scepticism about her heroism even while it dramatises the experiences of girl culture more widely: Wendy in 'Peter Pan' (Barrie 1911) and Mary in *The Secret Garden* (Burnett 1911) are also examples. Alice's Wonderland and Looking-Glass World are, together, an 'Underland' in which time is frozen, forever 'littling'

Alice and staving off the future in which she might grow up – a future mourned in Carroll's lyrics framing these stories (Smith 1993).

The full title of the second Alice book is *Through the Looking-Glass, and What Alice Found There*. This matters because what Alice finds on the other side of the mirror is a set of knowledge games collected into something structured more like a heroic trial than Wonderland was. Here, Alice must reach the other side (of a chess board) to become someone new, but Carroll confounds this expectation by again deflating the climax. There is no one else for Alice to become at all, and she less wins the encounters along the way than passes through them, learning only as much as negotiating that situation demands, even while she continually re-asserts her Alice-ness (Driscoll 1997). The resonance of Alice's dramatic encounters with herself is not displaced by the way post-1990s girls took on heroic roles. Rather, this drama of self-representation, where the girl remains at the surface of a confluence of forces and significations (Deleuze 1990), is integral to the kinds of heroes and quests involved.

What is most modern about Alice is the way her insistent agency involves consciousness of the limits placed upon it by the conflicting ways she is known. She offers a model for the modern girl hero's quest because her achievements seem so qualified, if not reduced to dramas of repetition, and yet there is no question that the story is about anyone else. There are, of course, modern girls who seem very un-Alice-like in a range of ways, including by differences of language, class, geography, race or ethnicity, age, education, and other variables that are not only about the distance of more than 150 years. But this self-evaluating girl identity, endlessly stressing statements about the self in contexts which question whether she has any self-worth speaking of – where she is both everygirl and merely herself – has become fundamentally *girlish*, even when taken up by boys or women. Otherwise quite different modern-girl types, from coquettes and tomboys to colonial and frontier girls, are recognisably continuous with this aspect of Alice.

Another reason for stressing this example is that 'Alice' is the first girl-oriented transmedia franchise. Following the books, Alice's story quickly became a play and over the following years was translated into books for different versions of a girl-centred audience. Alice became an iconic reference for ideas about girlishness in popular media, from political cartoons to Halloween costumes. Inspired by Carroll's stories, Walt Disney created a popular series of animated/live-action hybrid films called 'The Alice Comedies' (1923–1927) well before Mickey Mouse, and spent decades developing his influential full-length adaptation, *Alice in Wonderland* (Clyde Geronimi and Wilfred Jackson, 1951). While there have been many non-Disney Alice cartoons, movies, and illustrated books, the Disney Company returned to Alice again in the 1990s. A television series, *Adventures in Wonderland* (Disney Channel, 1992–1995), preceded Tim Burton's two updated Disney Alice films in 2011 (*Alice in Wonderland*, directed by Burton) and 2016 (*Alice through the Looking-Glass*, directed by James Bobin). And between these films was another series, *Once Upon a Time in Wonderland* (ABC, 2013–2014). Disney trades on nostalgic images of girlhood when re-adapting its female characters (Heatwole 2016), but the timing of this Alice renaissance is significant, with this series of texts re-interpreting Alice's blend of curiosity and self-conscious agency, along with her age, for different audiences.

While 1951 Disney Alice was a hybrid child/adolescent/young woman, the Alice of the 1992 series is a preteen role model whose interactions with Wonderland's inhabitants teach her about relationships in the real world, very much in line with campaigns for 'can-do' girlhood. Burton's Alice is very specifically heroised in opposition to Carroll's books, where she can make no difference to either world she inhabits, becoming a teenager surrounded by threats of matrimony but also literally a knight in shining armour. And Alice in the 2013 series is a young adult, also very much 'unlittled' and refitted to the role of speculative hero. These and other re-imaginings of Alice are informed no more by Carroll than by the proliferation of Alice stories and images since his books. Transmedia Alice is a symbol of girlhood tensions and potential transformations but also a manager of risk, including the obstacles of her own self-doubt. This evolution maps onto changing ideas about girlhood that have become their own popular cultural currency.

The contradictory attributes of modern girlhood apparent in Alice impact all the important girl characters in the Hunger Games, but we will close this section by noticing how they dramatically expand the role of a girl mentioned but not characterised in the books – the granddaughter of President Snow (see Figure 2.1). The books represent no girls in the Capitol, except as tributes or mutilated prisoners, but towards the end there is passing reference to Snow's granddaughter as a tribute for the new Games that Coin is planning to punish the Capitol's residents. The films make this girl a minor motif with, eventually, a developmental narrative all her own. Just before we meet her, Haymitch is visibly disconcerted by the sight of young Capitol children, one boy and one girl, play at killing with swords as if they were in The Games. This brief scene, inserted into the lead-up to the 74th Games, and lit as luxuriously as the children are costumed, concisely conveys the corruption Capitol culture imposes on its own children. But the recurring original scenes with Snow's granddaughter represent something else.

Figure 2.1 Snow's granddaughter with her family, *Film 3*

This unnamed girl appears three times, always in the company of her grandfather. In *Film 2*, she stands for the girls consuming Katniss in the diegetic audience, first wearing her hair like Katniss and attesting that 'everyone at school' does so now, and, later, wishing for a love like Katniss seems to display for Peeta on screen. While the gap between these scenes suggests a move from imitative play to romantic objects often cited in accounts of girls' development (e.g. de Beauvoir 1949), her appearance in *Film 3* suggests something more dramatic. As her grandfather announces that any reference to 'the mockingjay' will be deemed treason, the girl, lined up with her family as accessories to Snow's broadcast, and looking far more adolescent than one year would suggest, shows an immediate fearful consciousness of what this means for her, and quickly unbraids her hair.[1] While the plan for a new Games that would kill Capitol children always proved that Katniss was right to believe Coin would maintain the violent state-media complex, the passing threat to Snow's granddaughter is far more meaningful once she has been given this face and character. At the same time, these scenes collectively represent different ideas about consumption than the debauched excesses of Capitol parties. To read this granddaughter as a naïve consumer of images that do violence to girls by making them consumers is to ignore the way identities are routinely formed by imaginative identification. She consumes the political and romance narratives centred on Katniss simultaneously and identifies this as a shared social feeling. Moreover, what she admires about Katniss is neither simply inauthentic nor purely authentic. Katniss is useful to her – as Alice may be useful to those who consume her – as a manifestation of her own desires, however many Gamemakers, stylists, and commentators were involved in packaging Katniss for television.

'Everyone knows my secrets before I do': teen film

Given the books' use of first-person narration, all the production and meta-production scenes representing the state are original to the films, explaining events Katniss only deduces (or is never sure of). This transforms her story into one with multiple simultaneous locations and perspectives, as mainstream cinematic adaptation requires. But even when Snow's or Coin's positions are explained, we are never party to their thoughts and feelings, largely because both performances are so carefully impassive. Although Katniss does not always tell us how she feels, and sometimes expresses herself confused, cinematography and editing offer an array of close-up information about her responses that keep us engaged with how she feels. To a lesser degree this is true of Peeta and Gale, as well, and later somewhat true of Finnick and Johanna. While we may be surprised or intrigued by the actions of the adults, the interest of the camera is overwhelmingly in the adolescents. For this reason, the first properly cinematic genre to consider when analysing the Hunger Games is teen film.

As an identity crisis bound to both emerging sexuality and training in citizenship, adolescence was 'discovered' around the turn into the twentieth century at the same time as narrative cinema. This modern adolescence was viewed as a sign of both cultural change and social needs, and soon as in distinctive conflict with traditional cultural forms.[2] Teen film emerged around this distinctive symbolic life, drawing on fiction for youth, including new adolescent girls' magazines, but also on fiction about youth designed for a broader audience, like flapper novels of both the pulp and literary kinds. A new sense of the distinctiveness and importance of everything that appealed to youth became core to new cinema genres about and appealing to youth (Driscoll 2011: 9–25). Although what David Considine (1985) calls the cinema of adolescence has changed dramatically in some respects since the early twentieth century, the sense that youth involves a distinctive experience as well as specific cultural spaces and practices remains crucial to teen film.

While the Hunger Games films focus on youth, they may not initially seem like teen film. Some of the genre's current core conventions seem to be entirely absent – most notably, any reference to a separate youth media culture internal to the story world. Youth in Panem lack any distinctive realm of cultural practices and objects, and still less visible youth sub-group or 'subcultural' identities articulated through clothing, music, language, or other tastes (see Shary 2014). There are marked cultural differences between districts, but these also extend to adults. Across the franchise, districts are distinguished by labour, politics and training, so that 4 specialises in fishing but 12 in coal, 1 and 2 are richer and overwhelmingly more likely to produce peacekeepers and victors, and 3 is educated to specialise in technology. The books also stress other differences in music, styles of bread, and marriage ceremonies. But as the young do not move between districts except as tributes, none of these cultural specificities affect their relations with each other. In the Capitol, we also see no distinctive 'youth culture' between the play of small children and the stylized hedonism of adults. When *Films 3–4* introduce the director Cressida and the cameramen Castor and Pollux as young adults from the Capitol (they are less specifically aged in the books), Cressida's shaved head and tattoos and Pollux's beard do refer to young adult fashions of 2014–2015, but without any additional narrative support or context.

However, many other teen-film conventions characterise these films' focus and tone. They emphasise youthful romance, intensified age-based peer relationships (both friends and rivals), conflict with a distinct older generation, and the institutional management of adolescence by families, school, and other powerful social forces. Moreover, Katniss begins the films as a resentful teenager, alienated from the habits of her community and intimacy with her mother by anger at her father's death and the material injustice of the world. To the extent that she fits a teen film type, however, she is closest to the tomboy, or the tough girl who learns her value to herself and others. There are thus also remnants of a coming-of-age plot, including first love (although the Hunger Games evades the usual progress of this plot, as we will discuss in chapter three). Many other teen-film tropes are raised only to be thwarted, or even seem inappropriate to the story. Katniss's makeovers do not seem to internally transform her, for example, and there is no emphasis on virginity or relevance to formal education beyond basic knowledge. Although the films include images of passionate consumption, peer identification, and youthful impressionability, the archaically explicit mode of sovereign power that forms the dominant plot obstacle leaves little room for the peer-group crises of teen film. Nevertheless, while there are no high school cliques or street gangs, no house parties or illicit drugs, and the narrative resolution may be too ambivalent for coming of age to really dominate, the larger idea of modern adolescence remains crucial. The simultaneously physical, social, and psychological transition from childhood to adulthood, and adolescence as both object of training and subject of crisis, anchor the Hunger Games narrative. Similarly, while there are no classic juvenile delinquents, the categories of young tribal warrior and troubled youth are blurred in the 'career tributes' of Districts 1 and 2, and youth remain the right symbols for social alienation and upheaval, which is why the rebellion needs Katniss. Themes that underlie all teen film, including the rite of passage to social independence and the bodily and social trauma of developing a coherent individual identity, are woven through the Hunger

Games' larger dystopian narrative. If it is impossible to see a common youth experience in Panem, this is one key to its dystopia.

Encounters with mortality are part of the ordinary lives of district youth, for whom people starving to death in streets is not unmarked but not shocking either, and for whom a lottery of death dominates every year. This is beyond the usual limits of realist teen film, where encounters with death and intimations of mortality are crisis events, even in gangland dramas. But the heroic romance structure requires an experience beyond this ordinary world. Katniss is familiar with death, if in a more banally grim way in the books than the films, including the death of loved ones (her father), of neighbours (Gale's father, among others), and the regular massacre of strangers and acquaintances on television, and has even come close to starving to death herself. But being dragged into The Games nevertheless crosses a limit that makes her different, and not only in the eyes of others. Having returned home, nothing about Katniss's ordinary world fits in the same way, and nor do the ordinary people. In The Games, Katniss finds new doubts and new certainties about herself, as well as coming to an awareness of, as Peeta puts it, 'the effect she can have' (*Book 1*: 36). Peeta also is transformed. His first journey from District 12 to the Capitol marks the emergence of his character, unfolding him from an unidentified extra (for the audience) or a once-helpful but half-forgotten neighbour (for Katniss), to a master of public persona. Neither these skills nor his artistry seem to have been noticed by his family or neighbours, yet both help save Katniss and position him as a popular icon and an influential voice that some of the rebels would rather save than Katniss.

Arguing that the Hunger Games films are teen films supports the case against any '*mimetic* understanding of teen film in which teen film represents adolescence' (Driscoll 2011: 6). This is not, however, to deny the importance of the historical context from which the films emerged. If, as Benton, Dolan, and Zisch argue, analysing teen film 'is an important way of understanding an era's common beliefs about its teenaged population within a broader pattern of general cultural preoccupations' (1997: 88), then how teen film conventions work in the Hunger Games matters. The ideas about youth that seem most pressing around these films might, somewhat contentiously, be called *post-adolescence* questions, in the sense that they set aside the developmental certainty adolescence came to describe. While modern adolescence described an extension of dependent immaturity well past the end of puberty, this remained a naturalised developmental model. It proposed that every child should enter adolescence at a developmentally appropriate time (despite some uncertainties about when), and should leave it in order to become adults (despite similar uncertainties about when). As we have already suggested, many of Panem's adolescents are old before their time, some are never allowed to be children, and many apparent adults live in a prolonged state of unmodified childish indulgence and demand. This depends on the precise social conditions in which they live, as well as on individual experience, but it detaches adulthood and maturity from any clear endpoint for adolescence, an idea that has been percolating in teen film for decades.

Of course, the audience for the Hunger Games films is by no means exclusively teenagers. But teen film has never been a matter of assessing which films 'teenagers' watch. Early twentieth-century film industries around the world identified youth as the core returning audience for film, and this claim has continued to be made, despite changing times. Emma French has noted that a range of studies of young audiences, including a 2000 survey by the Motion Picture Association of America, acknowledge that the audience for teen-oriented films is not confined to teenagers (2006: 104–107). This is different from noting that the audience for blockbuster film, seeking the widest possible appeal in order to 'bust' the expense of an entire season's film bookings (once referred to as a 'block' booking in the US), must access this large market and so elements of youth appeal are routinely included in any big-budget film. The 'teen film' is different than youth appeal. It is focused on the liminal experience of adolescence – on young protagonists confronting generationalised challenges through narratives centred on coming of age (learning the way of the world) and rites of passage (becoming another self). Not only the psychosexual drama that runs through the films but also the social drama in which Katniss eventually takes a stand on behalf of the world in general, as well as those she loves, are typical of this genre.

Ripley, Sarah, Buffy: girling the action movie

The Hunger Games films are oriented towards action in their pacing, framing, and in the time taken up by dialogue-free action on screen. They often use special effects to further the plot and add dramatic content, and often use action in place of characterisation. Just as importantly, they depend on identification with an action hero. Katniss was always not only a girl hero, but more specifically a girl action hero (see Figure 2.2). The style of the novels is deeply indebted to a cinematic language for how things would be seen, and for communication without dialogue. The scene in which Katniss addresses the people of District 11 is exemplary, predicting exactly how it would be filmed:

> I stand there . . . thousands of eyes trained on me. There's a long pause. Then, from somewhere in the crowd, someone whistles Rue's four-note

Figure 2.2 Katniss as action hero, *Film 2*

mockingjay tune . . . What happens next . . . is too well executed to be spontaneous, because it happens in complete unison. Every person in the crowd presses the three middle fingers of their left hand against their lips and extends them to me. It's our sign from District 12, the last goodbye I gave Rue in the arena.

(*Book 2*: 75)

The books also emphasise sequences of combat and physical danger, leveraging the established success of the girl action hero across many media formats by the time they were written. Katniss's action-orientation has important antecedents, in the same way that 2017 *Wonder Woman* contains echoes of the story of Atalanta as well as the DC comic books, running since 1941, and the television series starring Lynda Carter (ABC/CBS, 1975– 1979). Katniss primarily belongs to the array of newly action-oriented girl heroes since the 1990s, but these depend on a transformation of screen roles for women from the 1970s onwards. Katniss and her peers – all those girls who heroically act on the world in effective and sometimes violent ways that we overviewed in chapter one – are inseparable from a renovation we will discuss as the 'girling' of the film action hero.

Opening a volume of essays on speculative television, Elyce Helford argues that, up to the 1980s, and for example in the figure of Princess Leia from the Star Wars films, speculative films had not moved beyond the recurring figure of 'the "plucky" but compromised heroine' (2000: 5). But, she adds,

> A few years later, film began a new trend of female representation within the science fiction genre, marked by tough, buns-of-steel heroines, such as Sigourney Weaver's Ellen Ripley and Linda Hamilton's Sarah Connor of the *Aliens* and *Terminator* series, respectively.
>
> (4)

In the 1970s, films like *The Exorcist* (William Friedkin 1973), *The Texas Chainsaw Massacre* (Tobe Hooper 1974), *Carrie* (Brian De Palma 1976), and *Halloween* (John Carpenter 1978) used twists on the familiar trope of the girl victim to renovate the horror film genre. That these are contemporary with other more physically active – but less confronting – young screen women, like Wonder Woman, the detectives in *Charlie's Angels* (ABC, 1976–1981), and Leia, should of course be tied to the visibility and impact of feminism in the 1970s. But Ripley and Sarah were heroes of a different order of toughness, and this type of heroism began to extend to girls in the 1990s.

It matters that all the most successful examples of this girl-ed action hero belong to speculative, rather than realist, genres. A *speculative* girl hero can act more violently and still remain both heroic and girl-like, given that neither her skills nor the dangers she must confront are checked by realist believability. One of the speculative franchises with the most influence over the increasing physicality of girl heroes since the mid-1990s is 'Buffy the Vampire Slayer' (the 1992 film was followed by a 1997–2003 television series and then a comic and novel series which is ongoing). The problem with Buffy, according to Helford, is that she may act heroically but her story also depends on long expected girl-centred storylines, including romance plots and related anxieties. This critique brings Helford to Carol Clover's well-known discussion of those new screen girls and women who fight back (1992), and to Elizabeth Hills' less-well-known reply to that analysis (1999). Because Clover's theory of what happens when girls (or young women) inhabit the space of action also begins with the 1970s, and because the Hunger Games franchise seems particularly ripe for a critique using Clover's ideas, this account, and Hills' counter-argument, are worth considering in detail.

Clover questions 'the "authentic" status of these heroines as heroic', suggesting they are 'simply mimicking the hero: a "figurative male"' (E. Hills 1999: 39). The example Hills and Clover share is Ripley, from the 'Alien' franchise. Ripley's role in *Alien* (Ridley Scott 1979) accords with Clover's account of the 'Final Girl' from slasher films appearing in the wake of *The Texas Chainsaw Massacre* (1974). That is, partway through a film that lacks any clear point of heroic identification, she comes to the foreground, and is eventually the sole survivor (Clover 1992: 41). Clover argues that

> the Final Girl is a male substitute in things oedipal, a homoerotic stand-in . . . to the extent she means 'girl' at all, it is only for purposes of signifying male lack, and even that meaning is nullified in the final scenes . . . To applaud the Final Girl as a feminist development, as some reviews of Aliens have done with Ripley, is, in light of her figurative meaning, a particularly grotesque expression of wishful thinking.
>
> (53)

Hills responds that this interpretation is stuck in a 'binaristic logic' where masculinity and femininity are mutually exclusive (1999: 39). By this argument, women on screen are excluded from a whole array of actions which are defined as male and which would render them only artificial men (Clover's – and later McRobbie's – 'phallic' girls).[3] Instead, Hills insists, 'action heroines' 'cannot easily be contained, or productively explained, within a theoretical model which denies the possibility of female subjectivity as active or full' (39) or by constructions which fail 'to engage with new characters and changing contexts' (40).

For Hills, reading the female action hero as tokenistic when she takes on traditionally masculine characteristics, and cliché when she takes on any associated with femininity, is an example of 'what Gilles Deleuze calls a "philosophy of capture"' in which the innovation of a new concept is contained and interpreted in an endless being-made-what-one-is-a priori' (E. Hills 1999: 44, citing Deleuze and Guattari 1987: 424–473). Hills goes on to suggest that such new forms of 'activity' are new 'assemblages' of, for example, women and weapons, and that new assemblages/activities practically produce new bodies (44). This is where Deleuze's use of 'girl' as a figure for difference itself once more becomes relevant. This girl, sometimes also called 'becoming-woman' in Deleuze's work with Guattari (1987), escapes capture by default definitions of the adult subject citizen.

This speculative 'final girl' is both transgressive and heroic through her own *self*-protection. However, it remains important that across the sequels to their spectacular first appearances, Ripley and Sarah Connor were not only made over into tougher-looking female fighters – very explicitly in Sarah's case, and accompanied by a far tougher character as well. They were also made over through stories of protective motherhood, as, in a sense, was Buffy, when the protection of her magical sister Dawn became more pressing after the death of her mother. Heatwole has written elsewhere that contemporary girlhood stories often collapse temporality to 'absorb motherhood into a postfeminist life narrative, which is necessarily that of a girl'

(2016: 17). The maternal roles taken on by Buffy and Katniss (in her protection of Prim and Rue, and her own mother) may be thought to leave actual motherhood irreconcilable with the youthfulness of the contemporary girl hero, and relegate it to her after-story.[4] When Sarah returns in *Terminator 2* (James Cameron, 1991), she is dramatically no longer who she once was, a warrior mother rather than a brave and resilient everygirl. However, the explicitly *girl* action hero also acts on behalf of others, and like Sarah from *The Terminator* (James Cameron, 1984) her story is often about her learning this is possible. The girl-centric maternalism of feminism from the 1980s to today (Henry 2004; Eisenhauer 2004) may well influence this typical story, and Buffy awakening all the Slayer 'potentials' at the end of that television series is also exemplary. At the same time, many of these stories reinforce reinstall motherhood as essential to the feminine *bildung*, and we will return to the fact that this eventually applies to Katniss too.

We agree with Elizabeth Hills that the concept of becoming is clearly relevant to the new gender formations apparent in women and girl action heroes. However, a caveat is needed. The girl heroism of Buffy and Katniss does not occupy what Hills refers to as 'a nonhierarchical state of pure difference' (45). Instead, she acts with explicit reference to the dominant hierarchical opposition between two genders even while evading full explanation by that opposition. The difference she introduces always *also* represents the standard it varies, which is why she can continue to work as a twist on generic expectations. It is often reported that Ripley in *Alien* was originally scripted as a male role (Schubart 2007), and the fact that the twist of discovering the hero is a girl still works for Katniss demonstrates the real-world continuity of expectations that girls are not action heroes. We do not require a theory of 'phallic' mimicry to acknowledge that the female action hero still intervenes in cinematic expectations; she is able to generate a narrative around her very revelation.

The youth which distinguishes Buffy or Katniss from Ripley and (later) Sarah also affects how viewers are invited to respond to their expertise in hunting and killing. We will return to the link between spectacle and the girl image, but here it matters that cinematic representation of the same action changes when it draws on the additional frisson of visualising girlhood. It is in dialogue with the pressures of visualisation we discussed previously, as well with reality television, that Katniss helps craft herself as the 'girl on fire' before she enters the arena. She assumes, when she first meets Cinna, that he must be there to 'make [her] look pretty' (*Film 1*). Once in the arena, however, her constant reflection on how she appears is not about her looks, or what she is wearing, but instead about what she does looks like. In the books, this interrogation of what people are thinking about her centres on trying to divine what messages Haymitch is sending through sponsor gifts.

But the films are more ambiguous. Sometimes she clearly considers what Haymitch wants her to do, for example when one of his notes hints that she needs to kiss Peeta more passionately if she wants real audience/sponsor attention. At other times, the emphasis is on trying to divine what is meant by the actions of other tributes, including potential allies, and what the Gamemakers and Games audience want. At the same time, in the arena Katniss is in her element, because there is rarely time for self-analysis; there is only time for action.

The primacy of action was always key to the hero formula and its emergence out of myth read as speculative fiction in the modern world. Vladimir Propp (1968) argues that it is *actions* which offer consistency between stories set in intrinsically variable worlds. As David Bordwell summarises Propp's point: 'Because the motifs or objects and persons can vary from tale to tale, only the actions – giving, or removing, or battling – can form the constants that trigger our intuition that two tales are similar' (2013: 9). The actors in a folktale do not need to be characters per se and are primarily effects of narrative 'structure'. Organised relative to discrete 'moves' or actions they form a 'sequence of functions, a distinct line of action' (10). Bordwell believes that Propp exaggerates the formulaic dimensions of folktales to make this argument, and that pressing it to discuss film only stretches the exaggeration further. However, while a combination of agency and mastery is required for any hero, the action hero introduces greater physicality and urgency, bringing it closer to Propp's mythic structure. The action film, when it does not prioritise action at the expense of characterisation, at least uses action as a key mode of characterisation.

Katniss stands for action. We do not mean that she is *action* opposed to *thought*, however many experts watching her within the story claim that her charisma is only apparent when her actions are un-thought. Rather, Katniss's action, which seems to escape mediation by television genres, fashion, or politics precisely because she is not thinking about those things but only about a transient goal, stands for immediacy. Katniss represents the immediacy of violence, suffering, affection, and freedom. Katniss is not only *becoming*, in Deleuze's sense – on a trajectory engaged by contingently arranged forces. To take up other terms from his work, she could also be discussed as a '*war machine*' in her 'deterritorialisation' of the state's productions of meaning; and she could also be discussed as an *event*, the repercussions of which make the conditions that led to it visible (Deleuze 1993; Deleuze and Guattari 1987). In all these senses, she is evading that 'philosophy of capture' which would reduce her to roles assigned by a dominant social order.

We do not necessarily need Deleuzean philosophy to see how Katniss's capacity for action constitutes a 'line of flight' (Deleuze and Guattari 1987) from the claims of the state and the ways it makes meaning from its subjects. Although primed for self-sacrifice, Katniss comes to reflexively understand both the symbolic power of that sacrifice and its pointlessness. Going to battle as the Mockingjay, one of her minders asks what they should do if she is killed: 'Make sure you get some footage,' she says. 'You can use that, anyway' (*Book 3*: 90). Katniss is not a sacrificial girl, though, but a hero who can refuse sacrificial and other symbolic roles, which is the choice she makes at the narrative climax. Katniss continually strives, and usually succeeds, to avoid being scripted and directed by others even though she remains constantly in touch with the judgements and values of others. After the end of *Film 1*, much of the Hunger Games' narrative drama is focused on forces trying to contain Katniss's action by translating it into something more amenable or otherwise channel or restrict it. She is rarely allowed to be alone after she leaves District 12 for the second time in *Film 2*, and yet she manages to act independently of any of these other, ostensibly more powerful, demands. While, technically, the sovereign state selects Katniss for likely death, in fact she elevates herself into this arena where she will become meaningful for others. While she does not choose, and is not even initially aware of, her revolutionary meanings either as a televisual commodity or a political slogan, Katniss knows that when she is reduced to her iconic status, her own character and situation no longer matter. This does not mean that icons are not effective stories or sometimes stories worth telling. Becoming the Mockingjay is a bargain Katniss makes for the sake of others – for a chance to save Peeta's life, for the happiness of her sister, for their cat's right to exist – but also for herself, because no other choice seems bearable.

Notes

1 In a deleted scene published on the *Film 2* DVD, Snow refers to his granddaughter as one of Peeta's 'rabid fans' after she calls wanting to meet him, before a meeting with Peeta in which Snow distinguishes Peeta's thoughtful reason from Katniss's, and by association his granddaughter's, 'destructive adolescent fantasies'.
2 This shift is usually associated with the work of American educationalist G. Stanley Hall and often with the new theories of psychosexual development proposed by Freud, which directly influenced Hall but also sparked both followers and antagonists in many fields and many countries (Driscoll 2009: 45–65).
3 Though Clover's and McRobbie's use of this term are not directly related, both they and y draw on Lacan's theory of femininity, for which any woman without 'lack' is referred to as 'phallic' (1977).
4 See Driscoll and Heatwole (2016) for a discussion of this point with reference to Katniss, Bella from the 'Twilight' franchise (discussed also in chapter three), and Lyra from Phillip Pullman's 'His Dark Materials'.

3 Team Katniss

In the arena of romance

The genres of teen film and action film that were our focus in chapter two have not yet done justice to the importance of the romance plot that winds its way through the Hunger Games films. This chapter begins by considering how these films adapt the romantic triangle plotline of Collins's novels, how they represent Katniss's scepticism – or at least ambivalence – about romance, and what they draw from the ties between romance, glamour, and developmental narratives about sexuality that are so important to girl culture. From this foundation, we turn to the dominant critical framework that has been applied to the Hunger Games films thus far: feminist cultural and film studies. This brings us back to the conceptual framework of postfeminism and the central question it brings to this franchise – whether Katniss should be considered a *feminist* hero. Does either the spectacularisation of Katniss in a blockbuster film, which emphasises the beauty of a young film star, or emphasis on her romance plot, compromise the film's feminist potential?

'The closest we will ever come to love': teen angst and bridal promise

Katniss's victory at the end of the Hunger Games is certainly not her achievement of a romantic relationship with Peeta, although this helps motivate her involvement in the larger dramatic political action. But romantic achievement does close her story, in a coda projection of Katniss's future that functions as an almost off-stage reward (Figure 3.1). And a romance narrative winds its way through the overall story, partly to explain why a family – two children with a young man she loves – seems an appropriate reward for Katniss. Understanding this coda requires, first of all, recognising the kind of cinematic romance that happens in the Hunger Games. Bound up with rites of passage – such as leaving home, and first kiss(es) and sex – romance in the Hunger Games is teen romance. Romance is crucial to the growing-up

Figure 3.1 Katniss, Peeta, and family, *Film 4*

story in films for and about youth, and growing up is equally crucial to romance in any such film. Learning to contextualise and evaluate forms of love is represented in teen genres as the maturing of sexual instincts, but also social skills, and thus important steps towards adulthood. These are also, in general, steps more important to girl characters than to boys. Even if girl protagonists do not complete what we could call *the bridal script*, and grow up through love and into a consummated relationship, their development is depicted in relation to this idea.

Sex seems strangely absent from the Hunger Games story.[1] The books never directly state that Katniss and Peeta do not have sex until after the main plot closes, but they imply that their many nights spent together are misunderstood by gossip because they are only offering each other comfort. The only clear references to sex are in the false promotional story that Katniss is pregnant, which Peeta clearly hopes will stave off her participation in the 75th Games (*Book 2*: 309–312), the fact that they have children by the end of the story, and the very loosely described sexual abuse suffered by Finnick (discussed later). Otherwise, the sexual relations of central characters are confined to kisses which are coded more romantically than sexually. Nevertheless, a sexual awakening is suggested for Katniss. In the books, she clearly marks a particular kiss as different than those performed, at least for her, largely for the cameras: 'There was only one kiss that made me feel something stir deep inside. Only one that made me want more' (*Book 2*: 425). What she identifies here as a vague, hungry feeling returns only at the end of *Book 3*, and sexual consummation is only acknowledged when discussing a conversation held 'after' (by implication) her desire has been fulfilled (453). Desire is not usually named as directly as this in YA fiction. However vague and indirect from an 'adult' point of view, these are visceral terms for the usually virginal girl heroes of this genre. It nevertheless is striking that the action-oriented Hunger Games films, bound by no such conventions, do little more to represent sexual desire.

One of the most chilling aspects of the Hunger Games story is the media attention paid to the youth of the tributes and the imminent loss of their future lives. But little is made of the sexual development that the franchise's audience necessarily associates with the age of those reaped for The Games. The *Book 2* suggestion that Katniss's mother might be opposed to her marrying Peeta so young does not appear in the films. More importantly, the likelihood that selecting 12–18-year-olds for The Games would produce sexual or romantic dynamics as well as violent ones is not directly raised even in the books. *Book/Film 1* each, differently, suggest an intimate (if not couple) dynamic between District 1 tributes Cato and Clove, and the *Book 2* recounting of the 50th Games, which Haymitch won, also indicates an intimate alliance between he and Maysilee Donner from District 12 (238–243). But it seems Katniss and Peeta are the first to attempt refusing to kill an ally in the face of Gamemakers' provocations and the promise of a victor's life. The unprecedented strength of their alliance by the end of *Film 1* is associated both with strength of character and strength of feeling, but not with sexual desire. When Haymitch declares that Peeta has helped Katniss by making her look 'desirable', this is framed as romantic rather than sexual desire, and even Gale and Peeta's rivalry for Katniss takes this tone. All of this is consistent with a continuing attachment to the conventions of girl-oriented genres.

Teen romance generally presumes that girls want romance and boys want sex, but one of the first scenes in *Book/Film 1* indicates we should not look to Katniss for romantic desires. In this conversation with Gale, Katniss rejects the narrative of romantic love, marriage, and family as impossible to believe in under the shadow of The Games. As Woloshyn, Taber, and Lane write, 'Katniss' critical assessment of the demands that are put upon her with respect to . . . the need for heteronormative romance' – as well as carefully curated 'appearance' – 'demonstrates their unreasonableness and, often, perverseness' (2013: 189). For an audience familiar with either teen or romance conventions, this scene suggests that romance is exactly what will follow, and very likely with Gale. Script, acting, direction, and editing all indicate a mutual attraction thwarted by fear of The Games, which not only discourage adolescents from anticipating children of their own but encourage pragmatists like Katniss to avoid strong attachments. But Katniss is about to be swept off to The Games, a twist which introduces Peeta as a rival love interest.

The problem of knowing how Katniss feels about Gale and Peeta hinges on what she does not articulate, but also what she does not know herself.

The films introduce even more confusion because they include no narration that could match the books' representation of Katniss's thoughts. They translate her general unwillingness to confront the question of whether she loves either Gale or Peeta – she does so in the books, but rarely, and never decisively – using the cinematic tendency for emotions to be communicated through facial expressions. But what is communicated by expression is far more cryptic than dialogue. As distinct from the narrative about Panem, and particularly the operations of Snow's government and The Games, the films introduce little new material to clarify Katniss's feelings. The only relevant additional scene is one at the end of *Film 3*. Having been attacked by a psychologically damaged Peeta, Katniss watches through a window as he thrashes in the restraints that bind him to a hospital bed. This insertion offers an emotional climax to the film, additionally necessary because *Book 3* focuses its affective drama on whether Peeta, and then Katniss, will recover from torture and trauma. But it does not clarify what Katniss feels.

There are three clear turning points bringing Katniss closer to Peeta than Gale in the films. The first is when she decides that she must die so that Peeta can survive the 75th Games. This choice is made in the wake of the first kiss she shares with Gale, as she is surrounded by the presumption that she does not love Peeta. This claim is reiterated by Snow, Haymitch, and Finnick – all positioned as people who might know Katniss better than she knows herself. Katniss's only attempt to disagree is when she tells Snow she is not 'indifferent' to Peeta, and he immediately brands this a 'lie' (*Film 2*). A second turning point is clear in Katniss's evident distress over what might be happening to Peeta after they are separated in the 76th arena. Her heightened attachment is marked by Gale volunteering to be part of Peeta's rescue team on the grounds that he cannot compete with a martyr. The last turning point is when Gale betrays Katniss's values by devising the trap that kills Prim, a trap Katniss has already rejected as 'crossing some kind of line' (*Book 3*: 216). But none of these involve any spoken statement of Katniss's feelings. It is consistent with her action-orientation that we have to divine attachment from Katniss's reactions and expressions. Thus, the changes that require the brief line 'Peeta and I grow back together' (*Book 4*: 452) be translated into a montage of adapted and original scenes that show Katniss looking at and living with Peeta differently.

Until this conclusion, the films maintain the books' entanglement of the question about whether Katniss loves Peeta with the question of how anyone living in Panem can know what is *real* (substantial, effective, unavoidable). While Katniss makes no declaration until the final minutes of the final film, Peeta's televised declarations of love are never quite disentangled from the storytelling premises of reality television. Loving Katniss might make her 'look desirable' to sponsors, but it saves *his* life as well when their 'star-crossed lovers' story sells well on television (*Book 1*: 135). Peeta pays attention to media coverage in a way Katniss does not, even evidently watching the replays of their own Games performance so that he knows how to paint Rue's grave in *Book/Film 2*. Peeta knows that audiences, sponsors, and Gamemakers 'must be manipulated' (*Book 2*: 426). The question of why Peeta does not himself need to look desirable seems to be answered by his statement that even his own mother thought only Katniss had a chance of winning. But the question of why Peeta is prepared to seed that image for Katniss is harder to answer without presuming that he is really in love with her. *Book 1* gives substantial space to Katniss's own questions about this, but *Film 1* uses the conventions of romance film to take Peeta's love for granted. After all, they are an attractive girl and boy, thrown together in a dangerous situation. Why would he not love her, even if she finally chose the boy-hunter next door instead?

Such generic cues heighten the narrative twist when Peeta, in the 74th arena, seems to side with 'the careers' in hunting for Katniss. They then offer additional satisfaction when he seems to help her escape them, and demand additional investment in her search for him once the Gamemakers have announced that two victors will be allowed if they are from the same district. Even so, the film integrates touching revelations about the history of his love for her with reminders that they are being whispered to a national audience, and Katniss herself is hardly sure where this commodified reality television story starts or stops being a survival strategy. The books allow Katniss to internally debate this, but the film adaptations rely heavily on Jennifer Lawrence's performance to convey Katniss's uncertainties. Without her internal rehearsal of arguments about what feelings are real, film-Katniss is confused and disconcerted by Peeta's apparent motivations, and her own.[2] Importantly, she does not know how to untangle her own feelings from tactics of self-preservation when *both* would be authentic feelings and the two cannot be clearly distinguished in particular experiences of pleasure, relief, comfort and gratitude. To add to this complexity, when Peeta is returned after Katniss has clearly suffered at the idea he is being tortured, that torture has produced a Peeta who hates Katniss, and believes all the worst interpretations of her actions and motivations, especially concerning him. This last twist in the question of whether Peeta and Katniss are in love externalises the larger questions about what kinds of knowledge or feelings are definitely real rather than just crafted expectation.

Finnick and Annie's love story works as a counterpoint. Finnick's media story since he won – notably as the youngest winner ever – has been his image as a sensual playboy with a chain of passing lovers. In their first conversation, Finnick seems to be both flirting with Katniss and taunting her for being too obvious when he says that, as tributes, they must grab any passing sweetness in life. His suggestion that he knows Katniss's secrets seems to be linked to her romance with Peeta, but means something else once he has been revealed as her secret ally in the 76th arena. From this point, Finnick's story is about gradual revelation. First, he admits that he thought Katniss was only faking love for Peeta, and now knows he was wrong – becoming the first person to say she loves him, including both Katniss and Peeta. Then he reveals that he is in love with Annie, when his pre-show interview farewell to 'the one' had seemed like his own media gambit. And finally, he reveals that his playboy history had been his own imprisonment, in which his body/company were traded by Snow to reward or bribe others. This reverses the usual gender roles in action film, where victims of sexual violence are almost always women, and he makes this revelation as a public broadcast when Katniss herself is too traumatised by Snow's cruelty to speak. Finnick's increasing openness is both part of dismantling Snow's power and a guide for Katniss, and his wedding to Annie marks the first wholly positive representation of love in the Hunger Games. Katniss herself is represented as an outsider to the wedding's celebratory tone, and this scene plays on her relationships with Prim and Peeta in ways that make it more than a happy respite before more grim war scenes, or a reward for Finnick before he, too, sacrifices his life to save Katniss's quest.

Romance was secondary in promotion of the Hunger Games films, which emphasised action elements and distinguished the film from romance-centred 'chick flicks' (Ferris and Young 2008). There is often romance in action films (see Tasker 1993), centrally as a reward for the hero or narrative anchor for questions about why the hero fights and whom they should save. But, consistent with teen film and romance dramas/comedies, the Hunger Games positions romance as a tool for forming a viable self, and a test of that self's capacities. While romance genres often rely on melodrama for their affective impact, teen film more often emphasises internal psychological drama, often as experienced by the kind of social outsider Katniss clearly is at Finnick's wedding. The *angst* of Katniss has three focal points: how to survive, and what parts of herself she would give up for that; what she should sacrifice to 'save' the world, and why her; and whether romantic love is real, or can be real for her. While her relationship with Gale becomes absorbed into ethical questions about revenge, her relationship with Peeta becomes increasingly centred on him personally. He comes to represent what she will not give up, what she must save, and what must be real. He is thus an apt reward for a girl action hero – part of what Katniss has 'earned', as Boggs puts it in *Film 4* when he, too, sacrifices his life to save Katniss. What she has also earned is that dislocated coda scene in which her life is both still and, literally, glowing with love.

'Dreamland': speculative fictions and girl politics

Rikke Schubart exemplifies a currently dominant argument about girl heroes when she argues that 'Today's active, aggressive and independent female hero is clearly a child of feminism' (2007: 6), but caught up in a 'post-feminist' 'age of ambivalence' (6–7) that merits feminist interrogation of its desire for fictional female heroes (12–13). Katniss's conclusion returns us to earlier points about the changing cultural expectations for girl charac-ters and to ambivalent feminist responses to their success and their happy endings. Central to this ambivalence is the sense that these new stories are, as Elyce Helford puts it, 'change without change' (2000: 6). To explore this point, it matters that we could make a case for the similarity between Katniss's story and fairytale princesses like Cinderella. While Cinderella does not risk her life to save someone she loves, in both stories the central girl's innate virtue, capacity for self-sacrifice, and refusal to be crushed by injustice are revealed by her response to the cruelty of others. Both are recognised and transformed by powerful people who can give them new and untouchably comfortable lives. The Reaping, the train, and the media extravaganza in which Katniss becomes the Capitol's darling 'girl on fire' follows a similar pattern to Cinderella's story, and both end with a glow-ing vision of future romantic domestic bliss that allows no interrogation. Such a proposition that the new girl-centred stories are at heart just like the old ones exemplifies one of the key arguments about the 'postfeminism' of contemporary popular culture. But Katniss is not simply a new Cinderella, given that her own actions determine the trajectory of the narrative and that it is her actions and commitment rather than her virtue for which she is finally rewarded. A focus on Katniss's role as an object for admiration (or manipulation) at the expense of considering her agency seems to us to miss the impact of its action-orientation and dystopian tone on such familiar tropes.

As Joanne Brown and Nancy St. Clair acknowledge, girl-oriented stories are 'often criticized for plot resolution that reinforces conventional notions of gender' despite having also 'enthusiastically promoted . . . the neces-sity for girls to gain control over their own lives by embracing their gifts, to engage in self-definition, and to use their empowerment to challenge oppressive social structures' (2002: 129). This tension becomes increasingly important as girl heroes become more popular, and critics invested in the critique of postfeminism have increasingly stressed what Angela McRob-bie eventually called the 'neoliberal' positioning of the girl as 'an attractive harbinger of social change' (2009: 58). Along these lines, Frances Early and Kathleen Kennedy argue that feminist ideals are subsumed in such girl hero narratives – winked at or implied by the physical 'empowerment' of the character, rather than dealt with head-on – meaning that 'girl power' rhetoric is 'shorn of its political context' (2003: 4). Anita Harris writes:

> To be girl-powered is to make good choices and to be empowered as an individual. These uses of Girl Power position young women as creators of their own identities and life chances, and as liberated by their participation in the consumer culture that surrounds them. They both emphasize the positive opportunities for young women to invent themselves.
> (2004b: 167)

A girl hero empowered by her own choices is thus suspected of compromising feminist ideals precisely because she manages to succeed in an environment thought definitively hostile to them. For her critics, if not her core audience, the postfeminist girl hero must negotiate a treacherous landscape of suspicion over whether changing ideas about girlhood reflect feminist achievement and walk a tightrope between arguments about how images of girls impact on girls' desires and expectations.

As we have already suggested, Katniss must embrace ideal images of both femininity and gendered heterosexual coupling to some degree in order to successfully navigate her dangerous relation to the state-media complex. She must engage with the 'masquerade of womanliness' (see Riviere 1929), which, although it may still apply to women in general, is today overwhelmingly discussed, under the label 'postfeminism', with reference to the way girls and young women attempt to manage their self-image. McRobbie defines the postfeminist 'masquerade' as a

> mode of feminine inscription, across the whole surface of the female body, and interpellative device, at work and highly visible in the commercial domain as a familiar (even nostalgic or 'retro'), light-hearted (unserious), refrain of femininity. It has been re-instated into the repertoire of femininity ironically . . . [so that it] does not in fact mean entrapment . . . since now it is a matter of choice rather than obligation.
> (2009: 66)

This involves, she argues, a superficial empowerment that relies on girls' and women's pain and self-doubt. Certainly, this might be a way to understand how Katniss's 'excessive performance' of girlhood is called upon to aid her survival in the arena.

As Jessica Miller writes, 'Katniss never seems more feminine than when she's acting as Peeta's lover' (2012: 154). This is the product of a 'compulsory heterosexuality' (Rich 1980) underpinning appropriately gendered performance in the society lived by Katniss's audiences as much as her own. This gender 'legibility', as Judith Butler (1993: 37), and McRobbie after her, might call it, makes Katniss more relatable and adds layers of generic cues to her character. Katniss's bridal experience is paradigmatically generic. It also summarises her relation to Panem society, which consumes Katniss voraciously, but through a narrative which is oblivious to her lived experience. It is apt, then, that Cinna chooses the state-mandated bridal gown as the costume which transforms Katniss into the revolutionary Mockingjay image for a state-mandated audience. It transforms Katniss from one generic subject position (the bride) to another (the revolutionary icon). While Katniss does not choose this latter role either, and resists it also, she certainly sees more purpose in that façade than in the bride.

While Panem society is not exclusively patriarchal, so that high-status political and military figures may be men or women, patriarchal values still have force in other ways. Many occupations seem stripped of the gendered associations a contemporary audience might expect. There are male and female stylists, beauticians, domestic servants, and technicians and labourers of many kinds. Moreover, femininity is not more indulgent than masculinity in Panem, and its attachment to vulnerability is qualified. A colourful ornamental style characterises the fashion, hair, and makeup of most Capitol citizens, with both women and men seeking personal decoration as a self-validating luxury. Girls are also represented as equally able to fight and survive brutal challenges, not only because equal numbers of girl and boy tributes are chosen for The Games each year but because the winners, too, come from both genders. That Finnick is the sexually victimised character, while Katniss is the strong, silent type, further suggests that some expected gender stereotypes do not apply in Katniss's world. A dominant dimorphic sexual categorization nevertheless has highly recognisable symbolic meanings, as well as considerable authority over social life in Panem. It is in this respect more than any, perhaps, that the Hunger Games seems 'postfeminist'. The fact that women can be president, or a military commander, does not alter the symbolic importance of performing femininity through relationships, including the tie between domesticity and maternity. This resembles what McRobbie calls the 'double entanglement' of postfeminist discourse (2009: 12, after Butler 2000).

Although one boy and one girl enter the Hunger Games arena from each district, making gender a fundamental social distinction from the first plot premise, The Games may be the least gendered space in Panem. Expected dress, hair, and makeup conventions demarcate girls and boys in the districts, and among the tributes in the pre-Games events – but for those about to die, these seem principally like costumes. Some female tributes have 'softer' skills, such as evasion, for Rue and Foxface, or Mags's fishing, but these are concessions to their ages and physiques. Katniss, Clove, and

Johanna are all weapons specialists, for example, and while Johanna wrestles only in the books, on film female as well as male tributes are featured in physical combat – and the most ferocious of the victors brought back for the 76th games is Enobaria, who has filed her teeth into weapons. When the current victors, Katniss and Peeta, formally display their talents to the production team, neither choose skills in fighting but, respectively, skills in strategy and representation: Katniss hangs a dummy and labels it Seneca Crane, and Peeta paints Rue in the grave of flowers Katniss made for her. Agility, stealth, knowledge, and tactics, as well as strength, can be winning assets.

The postfeminism critical framework always seems on more secure grounds with visual texts because it can find allusions to the spectacle of glamour, including the common conjunction of makeover and triumph. The spectacle of Katniss's action, from her choreographed mastery with a bow and arrow to the digital effects of her apocalyptic scene of action, can also be seen as a glamorous image. Katniss may save Panem from a corrupt government, but she does so in a glamorous outfit and on camera. The Hunger Games franchise has already attracted considerable criticism along these lines, principally focused on the pleasures of Katniss's makeover and the centrality of her romance plot. As these are both products of the narrative manipulations of reality television, such an argument positions Katniss – and identification with Katniss – as ultimately a media product. As Sarah Kornfield puts this case, the

> Hunger Games offers viewers an 'empowered heroine' who hunts, fights, and wins without a second thought for her appearance. Yet, the film's narrative firmly grounds Katniss's motivation in traditional femininity through her maternal instincts towards Prim, and the production elements (camera work, lighting, etc.) continually emphasize Katniss's traditionally white-feminine beauty.
>
> (2016: 5)

This reading seems to forget that the Hunger Games is itself engaged in a similar critique. If 'visual pleasure' (Mulvey 1975) adds something to Katniss's various princess and superhero-style costumes in the films, then the same scenes also insist that believing in such an image is a failure to be on Katniss's side.

Katniss understands the artifice of the Capitol's beauty/fashion regime – after all, it has been 'mandatory viewing' all her life – and her anger at Peeta positioning her as a potential girlfriend suggests that, however many girls win The Games, effectively performing femininity for the cameras connotes a kind of weakness. It takes her whole team's agreement to convince her that desirable also means power, just as Cinna has to correct her assumption that he is there to make her look 'pretty' with the claim that he is there to respect her bravery by making her 'memorable'. These tensions within Katniss's makeover signal its 'postfeminist' context. Rosalind Gill suggests:

> It might be argued that a makeover paradigm constitutes postfeminist media culture. This requires people (predominantly women) to believe first that they or their life is lacking or flawed in some way, and second that it is amenable to reinvention or transformation by following the advice of relationship, design or lifestyle experts, and practising appropriately modified consumption habits.
>
> (2007: 161)

In other words, makeover tropes encourage an image of girl empowerment as an embodied, and centrally visual, image. The transformations at the heart of makeover culture, by this argument, displace the subject and replace lived experience with what Beverly Skeggs and Helen Wood term the 'normative performative' (2011: 20).

Such an argument nevertheless needs to move beyond ideas about beauty culture. Images of girls on reality television consistently 'emphasize', as McRobbie notes, 'talent, determination, and the desire to win' (2009: 74). By McRobbie's reading, this image of the 'highly motivated young woman' is nevertheless a distraction, making it more difficult to 'discern real sociological intersections of structural factors of ethnicity, social class and gender, in regard to young women' (ibid.). The Hunger Games supports this concern, insofar as the injustice and poverty Katniss has experienced all her life are clearly obscured on television in order to highlight her beauty and character, or what McRobbie would call her 'colourful self-biography' (ibid.). It is what Katniss *does* that matters, and while how she looks is a way of speaking to certain audiences, as the 'propo' production scenes elaborate (Figure 3.2), how she looks alone is not enough – she must not only act, she must do so with sincerity for even her most saleable story to work.

The idea that girls can now choose between an array of gender roles and gendered practices, and that this makes any choice valid even if it opposes feminist principles, is one of the key targets of the postfeminism critique.[3] But there are other ways to talk about the importance of choice as a relation between gender and agency. Moira Gatens writes:

> It is the human subject's own choice how to read and use the cards she has been dealt in life. In some ways the card game is a good metaphor for the situation of the human subject. She cannot determine the conventions that govern the game, the value of the cards, or the hand she

Figure 3.2 Mockingjay 'propos' production, *Film 3*

is dealt, but she is nevertheless free to choose how she plays the game. Will she be defeated in advance if she feels she has been dealt a bad hand, or will she interpret it as a challenge? Will she play a 'safe' game or a reckless one? It is through the attitudes she forms, and the manner of exercising her freedom, that woman will decide how her body is lived.

(2003: 271)

Applying this metaphor 'in some ways' offers some accord between the materialist criticism most feminism requires and popular genres that speculate on other possibilities. Speculative genres represent girls' capacity to act as independent agents (against the dominant organisation of the world around them) as requiring both will and action. Choice itself is no more important than acting on that choice, and action is often required first, in order to create new options to choose. Katniss is almost always actively choosing a path through available options. This orientation towards action, involving a disinterest in fine political critique and a reliance on instinct rather than deliberation, might get in the way of holding Katniss up as a model of feminist action, but it also impedes reading her as a postfeminist masquerade. Katniss has no time for evaluating degrees of perfection.

The 'postfeminism' critiques would agree that girl heroes (of a certain kind) are expected and even demanded today, but also argue that they are burdened, even overshadowed, by an ambivalent relation to the impact of feminism; even that they are superficial satisfactions that make the dissatisfaction of living in a world that lacks gender equality seem tolerable. That this discounts any value in fictional speculation should draw our attention to the problem of fantasy in discourse on postfeminism. Staying close to the psychoanalytic tools, critics like McRobbie have embraced to explain the attractions of postfeminism, we might take up Butler's account of fantasy as a 'scene' rather than an image. Fantasy, Butler writes, demands that 'identification is distributed among the various elements of the scene' (2000: 491). The 'I' that engages with fantasy is always in the scene; not as a single stable position, but as one able to shift and even multiply points of identification.

At the same time as speculative girl heroes are often thought to fail the test of feminist heroism because of either their success or their happiness, they are also criticised for any signs of weakness (Driscoll and Heatwole 2016). Weaknesses, and limitations, however, are as important as success and happy endings to making the speculative girl hero work. Speculative fiction tightly relies on inference because any aspect of the imagined world which is not represented otherwise will be assumed to work like the world in which its readers are presumed to live. The contemporary wave of speculative girl heroes uses evident real-world limitations on girls' agency and self determination to add force to the obstacles faced by any hero. The real-world everyday anxieties and obstacles they refer to make girl heroes more compelling, at present, than boy heroes would be in the same story. This, more than anything else, is what constitutes the Hunger Games' engagement with postfeminism. It is neither incidental nor a failing that Collins includes, among the life-or-death decisions Katniss must make, such apparently trivial dramas as what one should wear, how to be effectively 'girly' for an audience, and how to tell if your peers really like you. For Katniss's audience, correct and effective gender performance is a powerful synthesis of knowledge and practice, the difficulty of which produces much anxiety, as McRobbie rightly elaborates. In Panem, correct and effective gender performance may save your life, and Katniss's resistance to – and refusal to be changed by – the makeover version of gender conformity is obviously meant to signify her intelligence and strength. The Hunger Games suggests that the most important thing in a world where image has become everything is deconstructing the masquerade, precisely because this is not how things should be.

The prevalence of the postfeminist critique in discussion of speculative girl heroes might be considered a form of utopian longing in Frederic Jameson's sense. Jameson (1981) argues that 'formal analysis' of popular genres – by which he means genres based on the heroic cycle discussed by writers like Northrop Frye – cannot be anything but historically minded. Such analysis must link 'the history of forms and the evolution of social life' (1981: 105) so that 'the study of an object (here the romance texts) . . . also involves the study of the concepts and categories (themselves historical) that we necessarily bring to the object" ' (109). Postfeminism in just this way is an historically determined conceptual apparatus that brings the girl into view contemporarily with the rise to prominence of speculative girl heroes. It is an appropriate frame for discussing them for just this reason, but we should not ignore the 'utopian longings' – the expectations that exceed any possible representation – built into this framework. Speculative fiction is always an experiment with the necessary terms of our present reality. Jameson argues that it is the 'very distance of the unchangeable system from the turbulent restlessness of the real world that seems to open up a moment of ideational and utopian-creative free play in the mind itself or in the political imagination' (45). We would press this further to argue that a utopian imagination of worlds in which girls can be heroes must problematize the known-world discourse of postfeminism. By displacing the complex lived experience of girlhood, it renders it subject to further interrogation.

Bella Cullen reads *The Hunger Games*

The Hunger Games is just one instance of contemporary dialogue between popular genre, feminism, and ideas about girls and girlhood. No text, or franchise, could fully represent such a set of cultural relations. At this point, then, we want to pause to make a comparison between the Hunger Games and Twilight – the only contemporary franchise that both rivals the success of the Hunger Games and has an equivalent focus on the idea of the girl.[4] These franchises both attest that, since the 1990s, girls going through the looking-glass are expected to represent more aspirational political relations to images of femininity, but they take very different positions on this. Twilight has often been condemned as a retrograde and even anti-feminist story (Silver 2010; A. Taylor 2012; J. Taylor 2014), but it certainly has some similarities to the Hunger Games. Both were highly successful publishing ventures in the YA book category, although the Twilight books also had very substantial success among older women (Dorsey-Elson 2013). Both place their typically self-conscious heroine in life-threatening peril that throws her resilient and intrepid character into sharp relief. Both feature a triangle in which the girl must choose between romantic rivals – in the case of Twilight's Bella Swan, between friend of the family turned werewolf, Jacob Black, and cultured outsider, Edward Cullen. As our subtitle indicates, she chooses Edward fairly quickly, and despite some intensity in her relationship with Jacob she marries Edward relatively early in the final book and fourth film. The Twilight and Hunger Games stories must be distinguished, however, on the centrality of this romance, and the questions about girlhood, sexual desire, and the institution of marriage to which it poses answers. A comparison between them shows the wide range of tastes and orientations populating girl-oriented speculative fiction in the early twenty-first century.

Many of the same audiences may well be engaged with these two series, and there are some clear overlaps in how they were consumed. For fans, choosing Gale in the Hunger Games, like choosing Jacob in Twilight, was to choose a different life for the central girl – in the case of Twilight this means a life in which death and trauma were not the prisms through which she became herself – and it is also to take a stand against some dominant generic queues for romance. An 'Unpopular Opinions' column on the website *Vulture* exemplarily makes a case for 'Team Gale' as the choice of passion over practicality (Dobbins 2013), and the 104 comments that follow (at the time of writing) map an array of feelings that took a similar shape in discussions of Twilight. Nevertheless, the most recent fan comment on this thread when we accessed it was: 'Wow guys. Just let katniss decide on her own! It's up to her and she's the only one who can make that choice so back off! THIS ISNT TWILIGHT!!!!!'

Katniss's choice of boy is an important part of her story but not its principle motivation or goal. Not only is Bella's romantic choice the motivation, goal, and substance of her story, but she is literally positioned as an ingenue who must learn her place in the world by this romantic orientation. Although Katniss learns important things from both Gale and Peeta, her strength is independent of them, and while Bella is always as brave as her love interests, she must learn to be powerful from and with them. Finally, it is destiny that determines Bella would not have been happy with Jacob. While there is little reason to think she seriously considers Jacob as a partner, the question of *why* fuels fan investments and adds tension to the middle books, until Bella's magical daughter erases the question – their attraction, it turns out, only foreshadowed the birth of Renesmee, who will be Jacob's true partner. By contrast, Katniss has a choice to make, and between people whose differences she learns across the story, including as they change and she does, too. We should not reduce Gale and Peeta to oppositional modes of masculinity. They are not soft and hard, young and old, fun and erudite, as are Jacob and Edward (Guanio-Uluru 2016). Gale and Peeta begin as attractive local bad boy and invisible boy-next-door-cum-supportive-friend, but these recognisable (teen film) types do not delimit them for long. Peeta breaks this mold almost as soon as the train has left the station, and once Katniss has begun to think about what kind of person attracts her, she returns seeing and thinking about Gale in new ways.

Twilight's transformations of the vampire genre are famously extensive. The carnivorous nature of the vampire, often read as a metaphor for sexual desire, is played down except in the context of controlling it, as when vampires remark on how good Bella smells. While Edward carefully controls his desire for Bella, Bella's desire for him threatens to (literally) consume her. While critiques of the way feminine desire is constructed in both contemporary media culture and contemporary sex education often stress that girls are held responsible for protecting their sexuality from potential aggressors, Bella is the one who presses the importance of desire and he is the one to exercise caution. While some see this as Bella ceding sexual power to him, Jackie C. Horne argues that this dynamic is in fact 'a relief', and 'speaks to a deeply important fantasy . . . for girls, exploring their sexuality without self-imposed inhibition' (2012: 32). While Bella may be a pioneer in terms of representing an assertive girl sexuality for girls – certainly more assertive and explicit than Katniss's slow-burning 'hunger' – this departure from convention is complicated by the ways virginity and its loss are tied to marriage and motherhood in Twilight. Traditional archetypes of morality are embedded in its emphasis on when and how Bella will lose her virginity. The main concern is whether Bella will survive sex with Edward while still in human form: a concession Edward unwillingly makes on the condition she marries him first. That is, Bella insists on risking her life for the sake of not missing out on sex as a key human girl experience; and she equally insists on valuing the man who sees sex as part of a permanent romantic contract.

Critics who doubt the bravery of these choices also often refuse to see heroism in Bella's active role in fighting evil and preserving good once she is herself a vampire. They do not only cavil because she had to die first, but also because her agency in battle as well as in love is directed to protection. As the song behind the closing credits poses it, Bella has always loved and been waiting for Edward, even before she met him, and this is what gives her life purpose. Her heroism is thus a mode of self-sacrifice. 'If your life was all you had to give your beloved,' Bella asks herself in the prologue to *Breaking Dawn*, 'how could you not give it?' (Meyer 2008: 1).

Bella has been particularly criticised as playing into stereotypes of feminine passivity, and it is often claimed that Edward controls her life (Taylor 2014). This is an overstatement. Bella saves Edward's life as often as he saves hers and her choice to become a vampire – made for the compounding reasons of being with Edward, staying young, and allowing her daughter to be born – orients the story around Bella's actions and desires. She is not just a fairytale princess waiting for her handsome prince. Recognising Bella's insistence on her own will is important, despite choices that appear conservative in the lived world of her audience. Bella's story positions dying for love, and other forms of renunciation for a life of love, as better (purer) choices than others that would keep her alive, and so fits very neatly that model of choice vilified by scholars like McRobbie. However, we should also recognise that Bella knows – indeed, every character in her story knows – that this is a bizarre set of choices, and even those few who know that Bella is in fact choosing to become a vampire rarely attempt to justify it. Her position is not idealised for girls without the vampire option, or presumed to make sense to her audience without this supernatural defence. Recognising this should also help us notice Bella's difference from most other contemporary stories about speculative girl heroes, including Katniss. But what Bella shares with those peers is a broad insistence that girls can bring about world-making change despite *only* being a girl. The narrative twist offered by the girl hero relies on acknowledging that the world in which they circulate (still) does not expect heroism from girls – and that ubiquity has not yet made their difference obsolete.

Notes

1 That is, for the canonical/official Hunger Games story. Fan texts, especially fanfiction, are, as in most fandoms, predominantly interested in romance and sex, and indeed often focus on making 'real' what is only possible in the canonical text. We will discuss fan texts in chapter five, but this is not our focus there.

2 In the books, Katniss repeatedly asks herself not only what Peeta feels but eventually what she feels herself. She wonders whether she knows why she offered Peeta the berries rather than kill him at the end of the 74th Games – whether it was to make whatever life she could have afterwards bearable, or whether she cared for him (*Book 1*: 451–453), and her plan to save Peeta's life at all costs in the 75th Games is thus linked to reassuring herself that even if that question is unanswerable, she clearly cares for him now.

3 McRobbie, for example, argues that:

> The element of choice becomes synonymous with a kind of feminism. But what the young woman is choosing is more than just participation in consumer culture. No aspect of physical appearance can be left unattended to . . . Such routine practices [pedicures, shaving, etc.] . . . are required by all women who want to count themselves as such, and these rituals constitute the postfeminist masquerade as a feminine totality.
>
> (2008: 66)

4 The four Twilight books, by Stephenie Meyer, were published 2005–2008, and the five film adaptations released 2008–2012, with the final book also being split into two films.

4 The train from District 12

Panem as dystopia

If speculative genres foreground dialogue with the worlds of their audience in pursuit of being *almost believable*, choosing the *speculative* label also connects science fiction to genres beyond popular culture. In this chapter, we are particularly interested in the dystopian tenor of the Hunger Games. The three sections of this chapter offer different approaches to power and politics in the Hunger Games, foregrounding how associations between youth, futurity, and both social change and social reproduction function in this dystopia. This chapter is thus also the one most concerned with the work of spectacle in the Hunger Games.

The problem of distinguishing reality from fantasy, from ideology, and from other kinds of image production threads through the Hunger Games, right up to Katniss's final choice as executioner. But this narrative turns self-conscious when Katniss and Peeta first board the train for Panem. On this train, we have a respite from new urgent problems for Katniss and time for the audience to become acquainted with Peeta, Effie, and Haymitch, and thus the political geography of Panem. Peeta is a son of District 12's merchant class and Haymitch its sole wealthy victor, and together they depict social differences Katniss (a coal miner's daughter) does not. Effie represents life in the Capitol through her disdain for the poverty of District 12 and exuberant pleasure in the train's luxuries, and together with Haymitch she also represents the difficult experience of mobility between them. This journey is a tour of cultural and economic relations between Panem's districts, the Capitol, and The Games. For Katniss, it also crosses a threshold: these characters are now her guides through the other-worlds that follow, and all will become her friends – although at first, that seems unlikely. Finally, this begins a story about what Katniss might become through the revolutionary war she triggers, although not without Peeta's contributions to inspiring people's devotion to what she represents.

'Perhaps I am watching you now': images of surveillance

We do not need Suzanne Collins's metatextual commentary to see that contemporary cultures of surveillance provide a visual language for the Hunger Games films that aids their *almost believability*. Reality television as a narrative genre is distinct from uses of surveillance technology for purposes other than entertainment, but as Susan Murray and Laurie Ouellette suggest, 'new forms of governing at a distance' are 'central to what is "true" and "real" for reality TV' (2004: 8). The almost magically unseen and unlimited cameras of The Games arena replicate at presently impossible levels the multiple hidden cameras of sets that themselves work as arenas on famous reality television franchises like *Survivor* or *Big Brother* (both beginning in Europe in 1997). Reality television did not produce these technologies, however much it has refined their use and reception. Murray and Ouellette further claim that 'Reality TV mitigates our resistance to . . . surveillance tactics' for governmental and other purposes (9), and at least in part, reality television tells stories about surveillance as well as using surveillance to tell stories about social relationships.

The Games in which Panem's youth fight to the death for the entertainment of an elite, and as a lesson in the power of the state for all, exemplify media spectacle. The series of life-threatening challenges set for Games competitors are undoubtedly real experiences for them, but they are just as clearly artificial and intricately stage-managed for political interests. In important respects, this is also continuous with Panem outside that arena. In the world that contains and consumes The Games, with its crafted personae of competitors who are also potential celebrities, individuals also manage more ordinary challenges by the careful maintenance of acceptable personae. In District 12, the Everdeens are careful that Katniss's hunting and the mother's healing services remain officially invisible just as the Mayor and his family pretend they do not buy Katniss's game. For surveillance in practice, acknowledging the law is as important as its prohibitions.

We suggested in the introduction that the youth of Panem are constituted within what a Foucauldian approach would refer to as disciplinary power, even as the corporal spectacle of The Games is aligned with sovereign forms of punishment. Michel Foucault's account of disciplinary power (1977, 1978) has been widely applied to modern educational institutions, and used to argue that modern social training centres on the definition of viable citizens by requiring specific social attitudes, with constantly visible possibilities for surveillance accompanied by status rewards for toeing the line, and penalties for stepping over it. The Games' tributes offer visible reminders that everyone in Panem is, at any given moment, potentially being watched, and the Hunger Games allegorically suggests ways that disciplinary power is deployed in contemporary media culture and otherwise acts on subject formation, including political consciousness. The conventions of speculative fiction invite the audience to recognise the relevance of this story to their own world, including both echoes of brutal sovereign power and the interplay of entertainment and disciplinary example. Yet, power in Panem is exerted simultaneously through military force and by controlling how people know the world. While it is not Katniss herself but the media discourse surrounding Katniss that begins a rebellion, it still matters that this rebellion takes place through direct physical warfare.

The dominant power of surveillance in Panem, where every action is potentially scrutinised by systems that filter up to President Snow, is particularly evident in the films. In addition to imitating reality television footage and deploying classic science fiction images of technological observation, the sets, editing, and cinematography of the Hunger Games films often refer to surveillance footage associated with security, police, or military forces. They often position the camera looking through, behind, and in proximity to such surveillance cameras and the screens representing what they see – sometimes as if the audience were ordinary subjects of Panem and sometimes as if they knew about the surveillance of Panem in ways those subjects cannot. The Games is not the only 'mandatory viewing' in Panem. Media power is organised in a centralised sovereign triangle when the story begins, bringing together many forms of spectacle in a state-owned and state-controlled single media source that closely resembles television. This resemblance is close enough that we have referred to Panem's single public media feed as television. But this technology is just different enough to convey a sense that this is where television might go in the future.[1] The 'public' and the 'audience' are identical for this despotic media system. As there are no competing programmes, there are no ratings, but as much as it is a form of punishment The Games is also a populist rally, and a more fervent audience following is equated with greater political control. This is not as simple as enthusiastic viewers meaning support for the status quo. From the earliest scenes in *Film 1*, we know that hatred of The Games is widespread in the districts, and the unfolding story also suggests increasingly complex viewing perspectives in the Capitol. *Film 1* summarises this in an original scene where Snow warns Seneca Crane against incautiously promoting Katniss fandom. The point of The Games is not just oppression, he says, but the seduction of 'hope'; just not so much hope that it leads to ideas about viable social transformation. The Games are themselves a mechanism of surveillance that looks at the audience more than it looks at the arena.

In *Book/Film 1*, from the perspective of the state producers, Katniss is just another girl tribute, although a particularly attractive one given Cinna's skilful styling, Peeta's promotion, her own charismatic bluntness and understated beauty, and the 'underdog' status of coming from impoverished outlying District 12. Crane's attempt to leverage this attraction backfires when Katniss finds a way to stalemate his planned climax. Instead of killing Peeta, who has been her ally in the arena and whose declaration of love in the pre-show interviews has built audience attention to their pairing, Katniss arranges what looks like a double suicide. Taken by surprise, Crane lets them both live. Although for both the diegetic and non-diegetic audiences, Katniss and Peeta's victory offers a kind of closure, the interpolated scenes feature Snow's concern with how this turn of events will be interpreted across Panem, punctuated by the implied execution of Crane. Katniss now constitutes a threat because her image is insufficiently controlled.

In *Book/Film 2*, using the threat of his all-seeing surveillance and right to kill, Snow convinces Katniss to collude with his media team and be represented as a harmless, adoring wife-to-be in order to quell the resistance she has inspired. This manipulation is visible to those close to Katniss and, although it is apparently invisible to the satisfied Capitol audience, Snow (correctly) believes it is suspected in the districts where scepticism towards the official media story is ingrained. The regularly scheduled 'victory tour' which takes Peeta and Katniss to every district, finishing in the Capitol, is a tour through attempts to represent this state-sponsored story, during which Katniss, Peeta, Haymitch, and Effie witness increasingly visible cracks in the Capitol's hold on the districts and their economic functions. Although the final party celebrating Katniss and Peeta's engagement still indicates general satisfaction in the Capitol, it also indicates these cracks are now the dominant concern of the media-state complex. While *Film 2* continues to feature little direct television footage, it increases views behind the scenes of producing images of Panem, where politicians and cultural producers attempt to manipulate knowledge of both Katniss's story and what else is happening in Panem (see Figures 1.1 and 4.1). These behind-the-scenes views imitate surveillance cameras more than reality programming until the 75th Games begin, when once again we enter an embedded story that blends televisual reception and cinematic action.

This speaks to Foucault's argument that while sovereign power comes from visibility, *disciplinary* power 'is exercised through its invisibility; at the same time it imposes upon on those whom it subjects a principle of compulsory visibility' (1977: 187). It is a blend of visible and invisible modes of power. Snow and his machinations are coextensive not only with the very visible *Big Brother* of the reality television genre but with the invisible network sustaining the partially visible 'Big Brother' in George Orwell's

Figure 4.1 President Snow's surveillance, *Film 2*

novel *1984*. In the Collins novels, this reference to Orwell is fairly explicit, but in the films it becomes direct through the increasing use of a close-up of President Snow's face delivering instructions to the public and invective to and about the resistance (citing popular recognition of Michael Radford's 1984 film adaptation). The cameras in The Games arena also represent this, adding televisually visible threats to the tributes' survival although the cameras themselves are only inferred. In line with Foucault's metaphor of the panopticon (1977: 202–208), it is never possible for the tributes to know when these cameras are being utilised. Moreover, they are connected via the production centre to otherwise invisible streams of information from 'trackers' implanted in the tributes, with this entire system used to impose life-threatening situations and heighten the probability of combat or other drama. While The Games is both public execution and a reminder of the need for vigilant self-regulation, the dominance of things to look at on the state-media feed is easily reversed, and during war the same screens become dominated by statements about surveilling authority and also literal executions (*Film 3*). The struggle for control of the state-media feed in the last two films is thus never ancillary to the revolutionary war.

The only time a specific Games arena camera is visible to a tribute is when Katniss detects and looks back at one, having heard its whirring from her hiding place in a tree (Figure 4.2). She doesn't avoid its lens – in fact, she goes out of her way to not only look back at its gaze but peer into its workings. This is only the most explicit of many times Katniss acknowledges the arena cameras in *Films 1* and *2*. The fact that she always seems to know where they are in order to confront their gaze represents both her singular command of the field and that they are (almost) everywhere she could possibly look. Despite Snow's near-omniscience, Katniss is represented in

Figure 4.2 Katniss looking into an arena camera, *Film 1*

such scenes as perceiving, questioning and resisting Panem's pervasive surveillance. However, as she learns more about the possible repercussions of her relation to such surveillance, *Films 3* and *4* are instead dominated by her attempting to hide from or use cameras, including hiding from the different but equally encompassing surveillance of life in District 13 and striving to voice her critique of Snow's government within the frame of the rebels' propaganda mission for the Mockingjay. Although Katniss's survival initially depends on performing an identity that differs from her own, this too changes. The 'girl on fire' persona is certainly compatible with Panem's hegemonic culture, but how Katniss understands her own relation to this persona, and to the Mockingjay that she rises as from this fire, remains one of the franchise's unanswered 'real or not real' questions. However crafted, these personae are not just lies any more than her inspirational declarations to Panem are insincere because she is wearing Cinna's mockingjay costumes. The politics of style and ornament are used to express identity and connection as well as for oppression, and they merit further analysis than the gendered dimensions we discussed in chapter three.

The mockingjay pin Katniss wears in the arena during the 74th Games becomes a symbol for resistance to the government as people take Katniss and Peeta's refusal to kill each other as a call to choose death over continuing to follow the Capitol's dictates. This symbol becomes conflated with Katniss herself as it is transported from district to district, displayed in graffiti in the train-tunnels that link them (*Film 2*), marked on pieces of bread carried by refugees (*Book 2*), or transmitted on underground airwaves (*Book 2*). The fact that Katniss rather than Peeta becomes this symbol, given his media popularity, deserves attention. The pin represents local resistance – the small mockingjay birds and a girl from District 12 – but it also begins as jewellery. In *Film 1* it is given to Katniss by Greasy Sae, just because she admires it; and in *Book 1* by her only girl friend, Madge. Either way, it is an ornament that marks her allegiance not only to the forest but to a pleasure in decoration now associated with girlhood. The pin is a sign that those not expected to take power might do so. As the suicide pact she proposes to Peeta in *Book/Film 1* makes Katniss neither the one saved nor the one who sacrifices herself, but instead a heroic ally, this turn against expectations is crucial. What Snow calls Katniss's 'little trick with the berries' exposes the fact that Panem 'must be', as Katniss replies, 'a very fragile system' (*Film 2*). Moreover, as Katniss becomes the Mockingjay – the symbolic embodiment of rebellion – she discovers that this role requires as much self-conscious performance as did The Games. As Kelley Wezner argues, Katniss 'moves from being unknowingly shaped by Panem's panopticon to actively participating in her own identity formation . . . It's not about what's *real*, it's the fabrication of reality that truly matters' (2012: 154).

Dystopia and spectacle

Katniss sees much that is wrong with her world, even when District 12 is all she knows; but unlike her friend Gale she does not itch to change it. Katniss in *Book/Film 1* has no vision of her own future and still less a vision of the world she should live in. What she has, instead, are valued private pleasures and a keen sense of injustice. Snow and Plutarch Heavensbee agree that 'She's not a leader. She just wants to save her own skin' (*Film 2*). But if Katniss is not looking for revolution in her choice to save Prim, and then Peeta, her sceptical pragmatic sincerity nevertheless makes her, as they also agree (although with very different motivations, as Heavensbee is later revealed to be a resistance leader), 'a beacon of hope for the rebellion' (*Film 2*). While Katniss stands for action rather than deep reflection, why she acts and for whom remains important. With the gradual loss of her home, private self, friendship with Gale, and finally her beloved sister, Katniss becomes less a warrior than the one who knows. In the wake of the rebellion's victory, she recognises that the world around her will only be structurally reproduced if one despot replaces another, and so the enemy she kills is not the now captive and dying ex-President Snow but the equally manipulative new President Coin. We should thus look more closely at the politics of the Hunger Games even if Katniss remains our focus – she is, after all, the Mockingjay, whose song reflects its surroundings.

In the introduction, we flagged the obvious relevance of Marxist theory to the Hunger Games. In Panem's political economy, the labour of people is objectified in the production of commodities valued on their own terms rather than for what it took to produce them. Consumption is a social and aesthetic virtue in the Capitol, and in The Games people themselves are subordinated both to consumption and to maintaining a status quo which keeps the Capitol in luxury at the expense of labour in the outlying districts. Panem, described this way, resembles the classic model of capitalism dependent on class distinctions and the circulation of commodities (see Marx 1976). People's lives appear to be determined by their different relations to the means of production, with manual labourers falling at the bottom of a hierarchy of both compensation and status, below a middle class of those who sell objects and services rather than their labour per se, and a ruling class whose work is entirely ideological. As in many classic dystopias, for example the citizens of Aldous Huxley's London in *Brave New World* (1932), the Capitol is placated by consumption, unable to see past formulaic excitements to the fundamental cruelty of their social world. The equation of Panem and American consumer culture in Collins's own comments encourage this reading.

At this allegorical level, the Hunger Games is closely aligned with a contemporary mode of dystopia predicated on, according to Fredric Jameson,

> the conviction that rich societies like the U.S. will need to convert to another kind of ethic if the world is not to end up, as it currently seems destined to do, in the spectacle of a First-World gated community surrounded by a world of starving enemies.
>
> (2004: 49)

Superimposing the geography of Panem onto a post-nuclear US emphasises this reading and activates a familiar trope for dystopian fiction since World War II. The books may be more literal about their placement in American geography, and most viewers would not associate the relevant set and costume design elements depicting District 12 with the Appalachian Mountains, although it was largely filmed there. But the image of District 12 is consistent with what the Appalachians have historically meant in US culture, and this includes clear markers of class difference. The films are, of course, also anchored in the US by casting American voices, well before the quickly displayed map in the background of a single shot (see Figure 1.1).

We might pursue this reading further using a later Marxist approach, to emphasise how the media feed in Panem works as an Althusserian 'ideological state apparatus' (ISA) that tells people what is acceptable, and even what is real (with the torture visited on Peeta in *Book/Film 3* being its repressive counterpart). Louis Althusser summarised ISAs as a

> quadruple system of interpellation as subjects, of subjection to the Subject, of universal recognition and of absolute guarantee, the subjects

'work', they 'work by themselves' in the vast majority of cases, with the exception of the 'bad subjects' who on occasion provoke the intervention of one of the detachments of the (repressive) State apparatus.

(1970: 180)

The climactic moment of *Book/Film 1* is thus when Katniss reveals the berries and stops 'working' as a tribute subject. Moreover, this reading is compatible with Guy Debord's account of 'spectacle' (Debord 1967) as the illusory world in which signs and commodities refer only to one another, detached from the labour and social structures that enable them. The Games is spectacle in Debord's sense, obscuring both its mechanisms of production and the realities of the actors within it. Indeed, Panem's version of reality television presents the apparent activity of the audience as just another carefully crafted product, as the faux participation that the Situationists and Debord associated with spectacle and opposed to 'total participation', which would be directly interactive.

Jameson's argument, in 'Magical Narratives', that popular genre is the means of expressing 'Utopian longings' (1975: 105), points to the same dynamic identified when Snow cautions Crane not to offer The Games audience too much hope. In fiction, Jameson and Snow suggest, longing for another organisation of the world can find representation. This can be sufficient to satisfy a passing fancy (Snow suggests), or manifest desire for a broader critical reflection (Jameson suggests). Utopian fictions are intrinsically political, from the foundational *Utopia*, by Thomas More (1516) to Marx's own work, where Jameson's reflections on utopia begin. Gregory Claeys and Lyman Tower Sargent also include Karl Marx and Friedrich Engels' Communist Manifesto in *The Utopia Reader* (1999a), where they define utopia as 'the imaginative project, positive or negative, of a society that is substantially different from the one in which the author lives' (Claeys and Sargent 1999b: 1). This not only indicates how dystopia is a type of utopia but suggests the way, like all fantasies, it is tightly tied to a framing world – although we would stress that this can eventually be the world of an audience quite different from that of any producer.

Having acknowledged the usefulness of this reading we should also stress that Panem is not, in fact, straightforwardly capitalist. Its workers are not all labour for sale, and its markets are not 'free'; they are organised by government planning rather than demand. The spectacle defining this society is, overall, less seductive than demanding – fusing classical spectacle, capitalist spectacle, and state socialist spectacle. This is emphasised in the films' costume/set design and staging by specific allusions to fascist monumentalism and Las Vegas-style hyperbolic advertising as well as classical Rome and zones of modern industrial poverty. The Capitol is nevertheless, as its name suggests, *capitalist*, with recognisable flows of consumer demand for commodity fashions. In the films, we see only the upper echelons of Capitol society closely, where all demands are met and supply overflows demand so continually that inventive forms of consumption are required to keep up – like the emetic drinks that allow revellers to go on eating after they are over-full (yet another reference to the Roman Empire). The books, however, reveal more about other layers of Capitol society, including Katniss's makeup team, who worry about how much things cost, what is in fashion, and limitations on supply, and the Avox slaves who perform the most menial labour. This team brings the Capitol closest to the America that produced it, while the Avox push it further away, stressing that the Capitol's capitalism is a literal slave economy under an absolute dictator who can both mutilate and kill on a whim.

Panem's districts all also have hybrid economies in which the fascist state centrally distributes basic goods in return for dictated labour roles and a limited salary for which there are limited goods marketed under regulation. The mix of distribution, labour, and trade clearly varies between districts, while District 13 is pure state socialism, with all goods collectively produced, centrally distributed, and labour roles assigned in a team effort based on apparent capacities. Everyone is provided for equally at a minimal level from scarce resources and this is evidently a more just society than either the Capitol or District 12. But the problems of 13 are not confined to having to hide underground for generations. The films split *Book 3* into two parts, but with an emphasis on military action that reduces detail about the regimented surveillance of life in 13.[2] The revelation that Coin would not be a very different president from Snow is thus left to hinge on her willingness to sacrifice children and healers to win a war, and to kill Katniss to negate her political influence. This reduces questions about what a Panem governed by this militaristic regime would be like to Coin herself, making Katniss's choice to kill her more simply justifiable.

None of this forces political or theoretical seriousness onto the Hunger Games, which was always a narrative about political power even when focused on media spectacles, lethal action sequences, or youthful romance. The films offer an unusual degree of political-economic detail for action fantasy. The fragmentation of resource production (one district has mines, another fishing, and so on) and centralised distribution means that in Snow's Panem – the one that excludes District 13 – only the Capitol can function independently; and yet, paradoxically, it depends on district resources. To support this distribution, communication is centralised in the Capitol and no cultural practices can reach beyond the most local audience without state sanction. Thus, like the Mockingjay symbol communicated laterally between districts by diverse local tactics, Katniss's folksongs become revolutionary. Transmitted to the viewing public, first from The Games arena when she sings over Rue's body and then as propaganda over the hijacked state-media channel, these songs are more than just signs of a hero's capacity for empathy and love. They are emblems of a life outside the rule of the Capitol, heightened by taking a pre-industrial form like song in an age of digital media technology. At the same time, introducing a crucial ambivalence, these songs only reach the pitch of communicability and popularity anchoring revolution via industrialised mass production, resembling the Nazi use of folk culture in Weimar Germany as much as the popularity of recovered and new ballad forms in 1960s alternative culture.

Katniss's songs are thus not peripheral to the plot, and they begin and end the film series. Each song is sung multiple times. The first is a pastoral lullaby, called 'The Valley Song' in the books and 'Deep in the Meadow' in the films (with a version by Sting recorded for the soundtrack release). Katniss singing this song to comfort her sister is how we first meet her in *Film 1*, and she sings it a second time to the dying Rue at the turning point in the 74th Games. The second song is one she sings partly to comfort her companions – in *Film 3*, the Avox cameraman Pollux asks her to sing to the mockingjays – and partly as a eulogy to the ruined District 12. 'The Hanging Tree' loosely belongs to the 'prison ballad' genre as the song of a condemned man, and it is soon taken up by amassing rebels in scenes original to the films as they withstand heavy casualties to bring down fortified government facilities, and Lawrence singing 'The Hanging Tree' plays again during *Film 3*'s closing credits. This song is a call to die with the speaker, but its internal meaning remains unclear, as the book explicates in ways the film does not (*Book 3*: 146–148). More clearly, it reinforces opposition between the Capitol and a seemingly more authentic pre-industrial cultural life. Even hanging as a mode of execution is starkly opposed to the technological spectacle of The Games and a meaningful archaism in a science fiction story. When Katniss is appointed to execute Snow, the apparently direct method of shooting him with an arrow is mediated by a production team filming it for transmission over the same state-owned media channel that carried The Games, only now under new management. This echoes the moment when Katniss decides she will do anything to stop Coin from continuing The Games with a new kind of young tribute. The song's ambivalent image of the noose as 'a necklace of hope' is also consistent with the ambivalence of the ending of the Hunger Games. Katniss's world is undoubtedly improved by the defeat of Snow, but neither Katniss nor the audience have any idea what kind of world she has brought into being.

The importance of the narrative coda can hardly be over-estimated in this respect. A new government of unknown tendencies has been appointed, and Katniss has been exiled to the recovering ruins of District 12, but this ending does not promise any more resolution to the problems of Panem than did President Coin. Katniss has won: Snow is defeated, she has returned home, she eventually has both a chosen partner and children, and she is no longer hungry or openly at risk. But she is not triumphant. The books are emphatic about this, detailing not only her ongoing nightmares but anxiety about what the future holds. In both films and books, there is a measure of freedom and peace in Katniss's new life, but it conveys little information about what Panem is now like except that it is not actively persecuting her. News comes to Peeta of her mother training healers, Gale keeping the peace where the peacekeepers were trained, and Annie's joy in the child she has after Finnick's death. Katniss, Peeta, and Haymitch watch a new president sworn in on television and remark that only Heavensbee seems to have won The Games. All of this remains non-committal about the larger political problems that the war contested. But the films give the very final scene a strikingly different tone (see Figure 3.1). Marked by shifts in every cinematic register, it is a soft-focus golden-lit pastoral scene with children playing and loving embraces that clearly echoes the lullaby with which *Film 1* began, and over which the last credits now roll. In fact, the shift in lighting, focus, and sound is so stark as to make this dreamlike ending rather questionable, but certainly it is a world of private reward rather than political solutions.

It thus remains unclear whether Katniss's success has changed or could change Panem. She has exposed forms of corruption and ended the repetitions of a traumatic history, but she has not solved its problems. The most hope the story offers is that someone (or ones) will be there to risk everything for the same critical purpose in the future. This also aligns with Debord's own utopian vision, where

> liberated from all economic responsibility, liberated from all the debts and responsibilities from the past and other people, humankind will exude a new surplus value, incalculable in money because it would be impossible to reduce it to the measure of waged work. The guarantee of the liberty of each and of all is in *the value of the game*, of life freely constructed. The exercise of this ludic recreation is the framework of the only guaranteed equality with non-exploitation of man by man. The liberation of the game, its creative autonomy, supersedes the ancient division between imposed work and passive leisure . . . So what really is the situation? It's the realization of a better game, which more exactly is provoked by the human presence.
>
> ('Situationist Manifesto' 1960)

We might consider here another account of utopia, this time as a mode of entertainment. Richard Dyer argues that entertainment itself has a utopian dimension:

> Two of the taken for granted descriptions of entertainment, as 'escape' and as 'wish-fulfillment', point to its central thrust, namely, utopia.

Entertainment offers the image of 'something better' to escape into, or something we want deeply that our day-to-day lives don't provide. Alternatives, hopes wishes – these are the stuff of utopia, the sense that things could be better, that something other than what is can be imagined and may be realised.

Entertainment does not, however, present models of utopian worlds. . . . It presents, head-on as it were, what utopia would feel like rather than how it would be organized.

(1992: 20)

Dyer focuses on the experience of being 'entertained', seeing in this pleasure something with more potential for disruption than mere distraction. In making this case, he offers another perspective on the overlap between speculative fiction's almost believability and utopia:

To be effective, the utopian sensibility has to take off from the real experiences of the audience. Yet to do this, to draw attention to the gap between what is and what could be, is, ideologically speaking, playing with fire.

(Dyer 1992: 27)

For Dyer, the spectacular effects of the blockbuster itself have a political dimension, offering an 'intensity' but also an 'abundance' and 'energy' to supplement the value of cinema itself as a 'community' experience, all of them (along with 'transparency', a key theme in the Hunger Games) responding to what he diagnoses as the inadequacies of contemporary social life (Dyer 1992: 26) and expresses in terms Debord would surely recognise.

The exaggerated closure of the Hunger Games may frustrate several possible readings of Katniss's heroism, but it not only fits Dyer's account of the possibilities raised by entertainment but also supports Jameson's observation that utopian texts 'bring home, in local and determinate ways, and with a fullness of concrete detail, our constitutional inability to imagine Utopia itself' (Jameson 1982). In other cases, this may be because the utopian text fulsomely describes its ideal world but not how that might be brought about, as with More's *Utopia*; but as a speculative dystopia the Hunger Games proffers no image of a better society. As Tom Moylan says, Jameson's theory of utopia 'does not directly invoke freedom but rather neutralizes "what blocks freedom" . . . Indeed, Jameson's point is that Utopia is not about this or that narrated alternative' (1998: 1). While speculative genres are often discussed as escapist fantasy, they often represent grim challenges to which there is no happy resolution.

'May the odds be ever in your favor': capital and the Capitol

The open secret of The Games, in a perverse reversal of its promotional slogan 'May the odds be ever in your favor', is that the odds are always stacked against the tributes. Until halfway through *Book/Film 2*, Katniss's survival depends on appearing to be a compliant member of Panem society because the regime that determines her life is maintained by two core strategies. The first is a stranglehold on all consumer goods, from necessities like food to the most fleeting luxury. This control requires manipulating both economic and cultural capital, in the terms established by the sociologist Pierre Bourdieu, keeping the poor and the wealthy identified with their respective places. The second strategy is the web of disciplinary power that leaves citizens afraid of any visible misstep relative to the status quo, including local regulations, unexplained changes in the code imposed by peacekeepers and, of course, The Games. Indeed, The Games unites these strategies, given that the reward for winning is not just the absence of death but a life without scarcity.

The reproduction of labour within Panem is achieved by exercising heavy controls on the circulation of all kinds of capital (economic, social, capital, and symbolic), but the most important is cultural capital. Without a sufficiently agreed-upon set of pleasures and values, Snow insists, the empire of Panem is 'fragile' indeed (*Film 2*). Bourdieu himself likens the functioning of capital to a game of chance in which the odds are only with the elite, arguing that capital operates as

> a *lex insita*, the principle underlying the immanent regularities of the social world. It is what makes the games of society – not least, the economic game – something other than simple games of chance offering at every moment the possibility of a miracle. Roulette, which holds out the opportunity of winning a lot of money in a short space of time, and therefore of changing one's social status quasi-instantaneously, and in which the winning of the previous spin of the wheel can be staked and lost at every new spin, gives a fairly accurate image of this imaginary universe of perfect competition or perfect equality of opportunity, a world without inertia, without accumulation, without heredity or acquired properties, in which every moment is perfectly independent of the previous one, every soldier has a marshal's baton in his knapsack, and every prize can be attained, instantaneously, by everyone, so that at each moment anyone can become anything.
>
> (2002: 280)

In fact, he argues, social life is not a game of chance, and success goes to the 'inheritors' or 'acquirers' of capital. Its great illusion is people's belief that, like The Games' victors, they might become anything, despite the real odds against a change of status.

The odds in Panem are clearly stacked by both wealth and access to training (terms by which the outer districts are directly disadvantaged, and by which real-life disadvantage also often works), as well as by the naked odds of having only one victor out of twenty-four every year. The transmission of cultural capital (of what one knows and knows to value) is key to The Games. As Bourdieu puts it, cultural capital is mainly passed on to the young by access to training or education (2002: 86). Within Panem's twelve subordinate districts, different forms of formal training are available and different kinds of knowledge are passed on through families. In District 12, the 'merchant' class to which Peeta belongs is more affluent and more attuned to the workings of Panem society, and has given Peeta greater social confidence as well as his other skills. Katniss's mother is seen to have sacrificed this class standing, and the accompanying advantages of her merchant family, by marrying a miner. Her fair, delicate appearance, inherited by Katniss's sister Prim, suggests a long line of maintaining such distinctions by bloodlines. Prim also inherits her mother's capacity for healing, obviously by training rather than genetics. It is significant that, in District 13, where class privileges maintained along family lines have been minimised in the interests of survival, Prim's nurtured talent provides a pathway to a medical career, while in District 12 her mother could only operate unofficially, paid by bartered goods.

In counterpoint, Katniss's appearance and abilities seem to be inherited or learned from her father. Her features are often referred to as the darker, more 'common', features of District 12 workers and she is also presented as sharing her father's interest in the outdoors, his exceptional hunting abilities, and his love of folk music (and in the books, his beautiful singing voice). These attributes associate Katniss with a mythical life before the Capitol (for the people of the districts) and by extension a life before industrialisation (for the audience). When troubled, Katniss finds solace in the uncivilised surroundings of the woods, a neo-naturalist in a world stratified by controlled urbanisation and state domination of media and technology (see Jameson 2004: 48). Thus, it is not formal education which allows Katniss to exceed expectations and become (at least symbolically) a revolutionary leader. Education seems to be mandatory and universal, but this is clearly not the assumed meritocracy of Bourdieu's or, still less, 'neoliberal' society. Following their education, the youth of Panem will take up the work that their family of birth and perhaps their gender assigns them. In Katniss's class in District 12, this is limited principally to coal miner (male) and mother (female). Like all other institutions in Panem, then, education works to maintain the current balance of power, rather than allow upward mobility, by maintaining what Bourdieu refers to as the 'conversion' of economic into cultural capital (2002: 285–286).

For young people of the districts, the only training that could change their lives is physical or weapons training. Katniss's intimacy with her father, and then with Gale, gives her access to such training, which is officially forbidden in District 12. Like the black market where she trades her game, this operates under the blind eyes of the law. Similarly, the military training of children in expectation of the chance at mobility offered by The Games is an open secret in the most privileged districts – the one associated with producing luxury goods (District 1) *and* the one producing the peacekeepers (District 2). These 'career' districts help maintain their privilege by aiding their children in winning The Games, and thus the health-sustaining bonus supplies channelled to a victor's district. Talented children are given special training and, perhaps, encouraged to volunteer. As fighting is not the only useful skill for The Games, however, the relevant specialist knowledge can involve more implicit cultural capital. Peeta's knowledge of how to address people and present himself is one example, as is the apparent ease with gender performance shown by Glimmer and Finnick. This all seems alien to Katniss, whose life has been dominated by the struggle to survive. Peeta's privilege helps him understand that they must provide entertainment as well as survival. He realises this means capitalising on Katniss's charisma and producing a romantic storyline so appealing it can overwhelm the pleasures of The Games as execution spectacle. In addition to knowing what will be valued in the Capitol, Peeta's command of sociality, including deportment, is a powerful form of knowing how to play the game. Although the class difference between Katniss and Peeta seems invisible to the Capitol, it is present in his greater social ease – what Bourdieu would call his 'habitus' (1977).

Both class and geography have additionally determining power in Panem, given that people are not allowed to move between districts, except in the service of the Capitol. Winning The Games means a comparatively luxurious home in the Victors' Village, increased income for one's family and community, a life of at least moderate celebrity, and the freedom to pursue elite pleasures, including travel. Very much like reality television competitions in the contemporary world, however, the celebrity assigned to victors may be a short-term benefit. It becomes increasingly clear that there is an ongoing price. Haymitch's alcoholism, Annie's madness, Johanna's isolation, and the sexual exploitation Finnick suffers, all attest that the repeated pain of mentoring new tributes is only the most generic way victors are indentured for life. Given that we never know anything about the personal life of the 'careers', positioned as trained enemies, we do not know if this is universal. But where we are given access to what it means to 'win' The Games, it seems that any promise of freedom in success is also a lie. The suffering of the winners also draws the Hunger Games commentary on class mobility and reality television towards Bourdieu, who argued that 'happiness' also needs to be factored into economic decisions, for example as a price for certain kinds of 'security' (Carles and Bourdieu 2001). His 'gilded ghettos' in which the ruling class are sectioned off from problems that feel pressing elsewhere seems highly relevant to Panem, including to the alien problems of Capitol residents like Katniss's makeup team in the books and the apparent racialisation of at least District 11 in the films – and thus of the key characters Rue and Thresh.

Beverley Skeggs, among others, has argued that what is missing from Bourdieu's theory of capital accrual is an intensive analysis of where it intersects with gender (2004: 22). She suggests that, while gender normalcy gives boys an institutionalised form of capital, femininity has a more tenuous position as it is 'a constantly transformable act based on attachment and detachment of practices and objects in a circuit of exchange, a wilful playfulness, performative and performing' (2004: 28). Skeggs argues that femininity itself can thus work as capital, with particular reference to how working-class women approach the performance of femininity as a form of social and cultural capital when other forms are unavailable, a dynamic she also sees in reality television and its consumption (Skeggs and Wood 2011). In this respect, Katniss's literal rags-to-riches story is both a hegemonic fantasy and the kind of independent success imagined by 'girl power', although it remains questionable whether it can be reduced to this label employed as a criticism. Like Angela McRobbie's account of the modern girl as 'an active and aspirational subject' (2009: 73), Skeggs' argument elucidates the affective power of Katniss's narrative starting point, which has her poised on the brink of both starvation and adulthood, needing to fight her way to fame and fortune by appealing to others as much as by being able to hunt and hide. The *almost believable* attractions of the Hunger Games narrative are clearly about a recognisable desire for something more than is currently available, but also about what blocks these desires and limitations, and is hard to imagine away.

Notes

1 Among the differences that matter, while utilising screens of various sizes that resemble television screens, this feed can also be vertically projected into the air and be visible against any background. Also, while this state-media feed has a signal that can be disrupted, and high-jacked, there are also layers to that signal which mean that while District 13 is broadcasting to Panem, disrupting a Capitol broadcast, Snow can in turn disrupt that flow and narrowcast a message only to 13.

2 For example, the abduction of Katniss's makeup team, and then their imprisonment for eating extra bread, is omitted. Rather than Katniss finding her makeover team starving in a urine-soaked cell, she finds her publicist Effie in a spartan dormitory, mourning her Capitol fashions.

5 'The Hunger Memes'

Film, fans, and speculation as critique

The Hunger Games films appeared in a context in which what happens in a movie theatre has become only one aspect of cinema, and in which the once tight connection between youth culture and cinema has been dispersed by closer associations between youth and other media. A presumption that young audiences are key to the commercial success of any major film nevertheless remains crucial to the Hunger Games. As we have argued, the Lionsgate films sought to leverage youth-oriented conventions within the blockbuster action genre, but the importance of the pre-existing fandom of the YA novels also needs to be considered here. This fandom brought its own interpretative debates to reception of the films, impacting not only the scale and breadth of their success but the kinds of marketing and merchandising that would work for this franchise. Moreover, the discourses on gender and (im)maturity that pervade fan practices are relevant to the life and afterlife of the franchise.

A now long history of scholarship offers widely varying accounts of what fandom offers fans, and how they relate to the objects they admire.[1] These range from ideologically blind immersion in the culture industry, as theorised by Theodor Adorno and Max Horkheimer in the 1940s (2002), to the integration of consumption into media production in the figure of the 'prosumer' (Jenkins 2006). Henry Jenkins claims he has 'watched fans move from the invisible margins of popular culture and into the centre of current thinking about media production and consumption' (2006: 12). While cultural producers have long tracked fan activity, in recent decades they have increasingly taken up fan media for promotional purposes in ways that complicate the relationships between fans, producers, and products. Whether understood as 'transmedia' assemblage or as signs of 'post-cinema' dispersal, fan practices of popular citation have played a crucial role in the Hunger Games franchise.

Rebels with a cause: youth, cinema, audience

Scholarship on cinematic images of youth has often focused on the way films reflect the changing experience of adolescence in the world from which they emerged. Sometimes this argument traces broad changes in the evolution of popular cinema, but often it is focused on more specific youth experiences, periods, or locations. As most spectacularly successful examples of youth cinema are American, most scholarship has focused on American adolescence, and the Hunger Games, too, is shaped by many American tendencies in stories about youth. There is nevertheless a more general set of issues at stake. Timothy Shary argues that cinema has seemed especially able to capture 'the nature of adolescence' and specially exemplary of 'youth culture', 'fluctuating on a continual basis with the various whims of time' (2014: 1). However, the relation between youth on screen and youth in the audience has clearly changed since the 1980s' 'Generation Multiplex'. As John Belton records (2014), decades of film criticism have seen signs of cinema's decline in new forms of audiovisual culture, including new modes of filming, editing, projection, and distribution. Drawing on Rick Altman's account of this 'crisis historiography', Belton argues that cinema should was always not 'a single stable object of study but a site where its identity is always under construction', dependent 'on the way users develop and understand it' (2014: 463). This chapter foregrounds relations between what is traditionally cinematic about the Hunger Games and its extensions into other modes of cultural production, from advertising to fan practices, focusing on the politics of genre and image that unite the franchise.

We cannot understand a transmedia franchise like Hunger Games by focusing only on its official published texts. Of course, we might analyse one, or the set, of the Hunger Games films without reference to the books, let alone to fan productions or the critical commentary that surrounds, informs, and responds to them. But what we want to call *the affective map* offered by the Hunger Games unfolds further than that, and draws its impact from elements beyond any precise textual component. We take the term 'affective map' from the work of Steven Shaviro. Summarising his book on *Post Cinematic Affect* (2010), Shaviro notes that:

> Cinema is generally regarded as the dominant medium, or aesthetic form, of the twentieth century. It evidently no longer has this position in the twenty-first. So I begin by asking, what is the role or position of cinema when it is no longer what Fredric Jameson calls a 'cultural dominant,' when it has been 'surpassed' by digital and computer-based media?
>
> (Shaviro 2011)

The book itself answers this question with the 'affective map' idea, treating 'media works' as 'machines for generating affect, and for capitalizing upon or extracting value from, this affect. As such, they are not ideological superstructures, as an older sort of Marxist criticism', like Adorno's, 'would have it' (Shaviro 2010: 3). Rather, such works 'lie at the very heart of social production, circulation, and distribution' and centrally gain their effectiveness from the 'affective labour' of consumption (3–4). Our use for Shaviro here is to stress that textual analysis alone cannot capture how films work as 'affective maps, which do not just passively trace or represent, but actively construct and perform, the social relations, flows, and feelings that they are ostensibly "about"' (6). Attention to what matters to expected and actual audiences is important for understanding how the Hunger Games films are affected by their generic, historical, and industrial context.

Images of youthful promise and rebellion have long been key drama for cinema. In numerous films, especially those seeking a youth audience, youthful screen rebels resist limits and oppressions in their personal lives, or built into the institutions that train and monitor them. Such films range from sex comedies to art drama. There is often, however, an inverse relation between the scale of the risks faced by young protagonists and a film's generic realism. For example, there may be grim personal consequences in youthful gangland drama, with a measure of social commentary framing the risks involved, but when focusing directly on large-scale social harm, realism is generally qualified, either by satire (*Election* [Payne 1999]; *Dear White People* [Simien 2014]) or by a measure of fantasy which allows young people to improbably bear the burden of social resistance (*Red Dawn* [Milius 1984]; *Tomorrow When the War Began* [Beattie 2010]). The latter approach encompasses speculative cinema and its televisual equivalents. Stories of youth in war zones are thus not often adapted to youth cinema. This is partly because of the restrictions on images of young people as subjects or objects of violence imposed by internationally connected national censorship and classification systems (see Cole, Driscoll, and Grealy 2018). These systems presume that realistic violence risks disturbing the young, whereas fantasy violence is part of expected genres for young people, from fairytales and comic books to film and television. Realistic images of youthful violence are also presumed to present dangerously imitable acts that immature minds are not equipped to put in context. A further reason for avoiding realistic violence is the generic convention that young heroes are singularly exceptional, which tends to exclude realistic war stories.

Both fantasy and realism are key to the integration of speculative and youth cinema. Horror and science fiction were crucial among the new subgenres of youth cinema that emerged in the 1950s, as film industries struggled with challenges posed by television and suburbanisation and strove to capitalise on the newly visible distinctiveness of youth culture (Doherty 2002). Both Doherty and Mark Jancovich (1996) have stressed the importance of young audiences for monster movies at this time, with Doherty foregrounding Hollywood exploitation of youth as its key audience demographic, and Jancovich focusing on its allegorical dimensions, including its capacity to represent psychosocial adolescent drama. On the side of science fiction, technology offered similar opportunities to speculate on selves, bodies and societies in states of becoming, as Elizabeth Hills suggests in her work on the machine-human assemblage as action hero (discussed in chapter two). Both monster and science fiction film have thus influenced how youthful speculative literary heroes are adapted to film, but the Hunger Games novels were not only science fiction but also gothic romance, and this, as well as their blockbuster action style, must be considered in any assessment of the films' audience. Speculative worlds are necessarily incomplete, leaving considerable room for alternative audience investments and interpretations, making such media works more amenable to generating dedicated fandoms. Any overview of fan hubs, on social media or websites, demonstrates how speculative fiction dominates media fandom. The 'endlessly deferred narrative' of sci-fi and fantasy 'creates a trusted environment for affective play' (Hills 2002: 104), which is both a draw for individual fans and the premise of practices that extend the text's scope far beyond its initial conception.

Converging on speculation: fan culture and the Hunger Games

From July 2015 to March 2017, a Lionsgate-licensed exhibition on the making of the Hunger Games films (Figure 5.1) travelled across four locations, from New York City to Louisville, Kentucky (Jennifer Lawrence's hometown), via San Francisco and Sydney, Australia (where both authors of this volume live).[2] While the massively successful travelling Harry Potter exhibition was its likely model (launched April 2009 and still touring at the time of writing), the pedagogic design of the Hunger Games exhibition was somewhat misplaced for an audience not centred on families with children. It was also dominated by a large merchandise emporium somewhat at odds with the franchise's political narrative. Despite such problems, there was much to interest us in this exhibition, which focused on production (especially costume) design but had a final room displaying the results of a fan-art competition. Most of this art clearly interpreted the Hunger Games through the lens of the Lionsgate films, but it also demonstrated that the franchise overall depended heavily on the fanbase for the Collins novels.

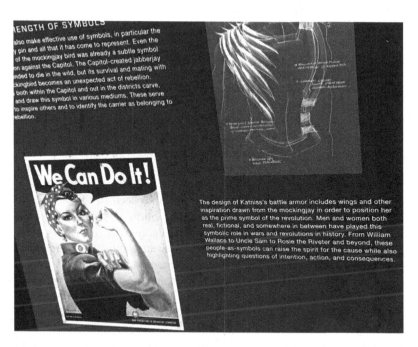

The design of Katniss's battle armor includes wings and other inspiration drawn from the mockingjay in order to position her as the prime symbol of the revolution. Men and women both real, fictional, and somewhere in between have played this symbolic role in wars and revolutions in history. From William Wallace to Uncle Sam to Rosie the Riveter and beyond, these people-as-symbols can raise the spirit for the cause while also highlighting questions of intention, action, and consequences.

Figure 5.1 The Hunger Games Exhibit (Sydney, December 2016)

The Hunger Games Fandom Wiki (http://thehungergames.wikia.com) has had a much longer life, beginning with fans of the books and still generating daily updates to its fan feed. Like other Hunger Games fansites, it indicates overall consistency with the workings of other popular media fandoms. Shared knowledge is key, including knowledge accumulation like this wiki, which juxtaposes the novels and films while also distinguishing between them, and features fan shorthands like 'D12' for District 12. Socialisation is also important, including social media links. In fan productions, the usual pairing attachments and related conventions are apparent, demonstrating diverse and sometimes competing interpretations of the narrative. While most fan paraphernalia (licenced and otherwise) focuses on Katniss, fanfiction always encourages specialisation, niche subcommunities, and experiments with story variation. Disagreements are thus as important as consensus (Johnson 2007), including over the correct pairing for Katniss, or even what to call key 'ships' (short for relationships). For example, serious Katniss/Peeta shippers tend to use Everlark, but Peeniss is also used, usually to satirise the pairing.[3] While the films now dominate visualisation of the story, the differences they introduced are frequently marked, and widely disparaged in some fan communities even as fan knowledge has sometimes been overtaken by the films and canonised by Collins's role as co-producer. One example is speculation over how the map of Panem would exactly correspond to the contemporary US, which *Film 2* ended with the authorised map (Figure 1.1) that was then incorporated into the exhibition.

The pleasure in exhaustively knowing a world which attracts fans to speculative fiction strengthens associations between fandom and immaturity, but the pleasure in textual immersion and shared passion has also been particularly associated with women (e.g. Radway 1984). As Joli Jensen points out, there have long been two dominant images of the fan – 'the obsessed individual and the hysterical crowd' (1992: 9) – respectively associated with youth and femininity. Girls have thus seemed like archetypal fans, as in Adorno, or in later studies of pop music and fanfiction (Hills 2002: 73), although many devoted fans are actually older women, even for YA franchises (e.g. Dorsey-Elson 2013). Jensen argues that the pathologisation of fans which sees them as immature 'is based in, supports, and justifies elitist and disrespectful beliefs about our common life' and cuts us 'off from understanding how value and meaning are enacted and shared in contemporary life' (1992: 26). But while taking fan practices as key elements of the Hunger Games franchise aligns with some key tenets of media studies, blockbuster films have also typified another kind of hierarchy – a critical framework that positions 'spectacle versus narrative' and 'merchandizing versus authentic art', with 'each opposition [restaging] a clash between valued culture and devalued economy' (Hills 2003: 181). The presumption that the appeal of blockbusters is ephemeral and inauthentic is shifted by a fan focus given that the 'cult blockbuster' is built on durable fan investments (182) rather than being merely an ' "event" movie' (183).

The blockbuster category gained new currency in the 1970s and 1980s, referring to massively successful films such as *Jaws* (Spielberg 1975) and *Die Hard* (McTiernan 1988), redefined, as Geoff King argues, by their 'intensity' and 'abundance' (2003: 118) – terms he takes from Richard Dyer's account of entertainment film utopia discussed in chapter four. They also had at least a superlative relation to realism. Action and speculative film genres each provide additional opportunities for intense and abundant special effects. Fantasy and science fiction themselves emphasise novelty, while also offering additional rewards for fans who collectivise around interpretation of media works, and are in turn inclined to repeat viewings and an array of profit or publicity-generating fan activities (Jenkins 2006). While t-shirts and posters have been licenced to promote *Jaws* and *Die Hard*, authorised merchandising for the Hunger Games was not only much broader but prioritised youth, from dolls (Figure 0.1) and school supplies to makeup ranges. The youth- and female-oriented demographics of the franchise's durable fanbase is also evident in fan productions shared, traded, and sold among fans.

Although fans have often been viewed as obsessive, and have often regarded themselves as gatekeepers to properly discriminating appreciation of their fan objects (Hills 2002), recent scholarship has followed the lead of writers like Hills and Jenkins in stressing the increased intersection of consumer/fan roles and consumer/producer roles. 'While simultaneously "resisting" norms of capitalist society and its rapid turnover of novel commodity,' writes Hills, 'fans are also implicated in those very economic and cultural processes' and the conventional opposition 'between the "fan" and the "consumer", falsifies the fan's experience by positioning fan and consumer as separable cultural identities' (2002: 29). Jenkins further complicates producer/consumer oppositions by focusing on the diverse ways producers now aim to engage fan attachment, and all these complications are apparent in fan relations to the Lionsgate films. They are also shaped, for many fans, by the Hunger Games' internal story about the politics of media consumption.

An impressively diverse range of Hunger Games fan productions is (still) available on hubs like etsy, redbubble, or cafepress, or tagged on Pinterest: replica costumes and accessories from the films; fan art on myriad surfaces, from posters to water bottles and phone cases; clothing and accessories bearing images from or commentary on the books/films; and homewares like cushions, bath salts, and cookie cutters. The crossovers between fan-product and producer-product to which Jenkins points in *Convergence Culture* (2006) are very apparent, including licencing of a Hunger Games 'store' on cafepress and, perhaps most significantly, the forms of fan interactivity built into Lionsgate's promotional website, *Capitol.pn*, which even coined a URL extension for the nation of Panem (see frontispiece).[4] Lionsgate courted fans in complex ways through this site, which leveraged an extensive fanbase using proven digital fan-exploitation tactics. A key entry point to *Capitol.pn* was assignment of an official ID that allocated that user a home 'district'. While the 'sorting hat' on the Harry Potter fan extension site, Pottermore (www.pottermore.com), requires answers to a quiz, ostensibly reflecting the user's personality, *Capitol.pn* replicated Panem's structural inequity and randomly assigned these districts. Once a member, fans could learn more about their district (and others) and also read the polished design magazine *Capitol Couture*, which featured the work of costume, makeup, and set designers, while also reflecting the hyper-stylised lifestyle of Capitol residents.

The *Capitol.pn* site changed to match the film series narrative – first becoming an explicit propaganda tool for President Snow, but eventually taken over by the rebels and renamed *resistance.pn* (the frontsipiece uses one of the new images this involved). New participatory elements were also introduced across this campaign, from hashtags like #ohsocapitol to the opportunity to digitally tag buildings with Mockingjay symbols (Bourdaa 2016: 96). Hannah Mueller credits the commercial acumen and fan engagement in this strategy:

> This kind of storytelling across different media requires audiences to trace all the narrative threads on different platforms if they want to feel like they have all the relevant knowledge, and it rewards those who do with the feeling of being part of an interpretative community of insiders. At the same time, transmedia storytelling facilitates brand loyalty, because it forces consumers to engage with or buy different products associated with the brand.
>
> (2017: 140)

Content was often linked to additional opportunities for fan consumption, so that, for example, Katniss's superficial branding as a fashion designer within the *Book/Film 2* storyline was linked to a licenced clothing line available for purchase (Bourdaa 2016: 95).

Many fans responded positively, with sites like 'Welcome to District 12' excitedly tracking changes (www.welcometodistrict12.com/p/communic uff.html). But as the fan commentary on Tumblr scrolling down the side of that site indicates, fans also debated the appropriateness of such marketing. Melanie Bourdaa stresses antagonism between the *Capitol.pn* channelling of fan enthusiasm and what she calls 'fan activism', by which 'fans "took back the narratives" and focused their energies towards something more meaningful to them' (2016: 90). This included objecting to appropriation of fans' local activities to promote the Lionsgate product in ways that ironically mirrored how the Capitol uses the lives of district tributes. Bourdaa particularly targets 'fanadvertising' – content produced by fans, like hashtagged Instagram photos, and incorporated into the campaign as a form of unpaid 'digital labour' (100). Both Mueller and Bourdaa note real-world activists using the three-finger salute popularised by Katniss, sometimes with serious consequences. But fan activism more usually focused on articulating links between the story and real-world politics. Bourdaa highlights the Harry Potter Alliance's campaign, which used the Hunger Games films to promote consciousness of poverty and hunger: tackling 'economic inequality on several levels as well as the disparity between the Hunger Games franchise's poignant content and its vapid, exploitative marketing strategy' (The Harry Potter Alliance 2015). HPA's message that 'the hunger games are real' belonged to a broader position, addressing many fandoms, that 'fantasy is not only an escape from our world, but an invitation to go deeper into it' (2015). Their Tumblr campaign, like Capitol.pn, mirrored the structural impoverishment of the districts, being

> divided into 12 sections, echoing the 12 districts of Panem: access to healthcare, to households, to education, gender equalities, environment, violence . . . After choosing a cause to defend, fans were then given precise, concrete action plans to follow, which were written by dedicated fans.
>
> (Bourdaa 2016: 100)

Bourdaa is right to say the *Capitol.pn* campaign focused on the 'glamour' of the Capitol rather than the 'roughness' of the districts or The Games. But, as the exhibition stressed, this site was meant to be read as initially manifesting the perspective of the Capitol:

> The District Heroes and District Voices campaigns in turn highlighted the Capitol's vision of the districts. They feature noble, hard-working, and loyally patriotic citizens who take pride in the products their homes provide for the good of Panem and who unquestioningly welcome and follow the wisdom and guidance of their leader, President Snow.
>
> (Lionsgate 2017)

The rewriting of the Capitol.pn, as the rebels won and displaced Capitol propaganda with their own, was not as visible as the viral pleasures or antagonisms of the Capitol Couture photoshoots. Similarly, the site's clear references to fascist iconography, as well the surrealism of couture fashion, often disappeared in the wider circulation of its images.

Lionsgate marketing/merchandising attempted to interpellate fans of the story's critique of consumption and propagandistic control as well as less self-consciously critical fans. Collins weighed in on the subsequent debate to flag this ambivalence as part of the adaptation:

> The stunning image of Katniss in her wedding dress that we use to sell tickets is just the kind of thing the Capitol would use to rev up its audience for the Quarter Quell . . . That dualistic approach is very much in keeping with the books.
>
> (quoted in Graser 2013)

While meta-fandom sites like *The Mary Sue* overviewed the best and most innovative Hunger Games merchandise (Polo 2012), offering both positive and negative perspectives, other fans did not always take such self-reflexivity as a sufficient defence. On an advertisement for CoverGirl's Capitol Collection makeup sets framed as 'Get Your Bougie Capitol Self Some Hunger Games Makeup', one fan protested that they 'didn't think anything could miss the point worse than Great Gatsby-themed parties or The Help-themed cookware' (Dries 2013).

'Jennifer Lawrence'

One of the most faithful elements of the Hunger Games film adaptations is the way they translate Katniss's first-person narration into the identificatory figure of movie star Jennifer Lawrence. At the time *Film 1* was cast, Lawrence was still a new face, and cinematographic emphasis on her youthful appeal was key to keeping Katniss at the heart of the films even in the most spectacular action sequences. It would be a mistake to discuss the Hunger Games without considering Lawrence's role in its success.

Studies of stars and fandom have noted the difficulty of converting child or adolescent stardom into adult stardom (O'Connor 2010). Since there have been recognisable youth film genres, young stars have struggled to continue that fame in later years: Mary Pickford, Clara Bow, Shirley Temple, Sandra Dee, Tatum O'Neal, Molly Ringwald, Lindsay Lohan. There are youth cinema stars who continued on to outstanding adult careers, including Mickey Rooney, Johnny Depp, Leonardo DiCaprio, Jake Gyllenhaal, Ron Howard, and Sean Penn. But even where art film and youth drama overlap this more rarely happens for girl-stars, and Lawrence belongs among the obvious exceptions, with Sally Field, Jodie Foster, and Drew Barrymore. Around the time she was cast in the Hunger Games, Lawrence was also cast in *Silver Linings Playbook* (Russell 2012), for which she won an Academy Award, a Golden Globe, and a Screen Actors Guild award, among others. The director of that film, David O. Russell, has come to represent a crossover point between mainstream and art film success, and so has Lawrence. During the 2011–2012 season in which she won these awards, Lawrence not only featured in *Film 1* but in another blockbuster speculative film, *X-Men: First Class* (Vaughn 2011), as well as other films that continue to be less known. Lawrence was cast for all three star-making films on the back of a relatively small-budget success, *Winter's Bone* (2010), written and directed by Debra Granik, where, as in the bigger films, Lawrence plays a young, wily survivor. While filming for the Hunger Games series, Lawrence continued to play more acclaimed roles in dramatic films, like *American Hustle* (Russell 2013) and *Joy* (Russell 2015), but Katniss remains a signature role and her most financially successful in box-office terms – although not for her personally, as we will discuss later.

In March 2011, then, when the casting of Katniss was announced, a combination of relative newness and an established fanbase led inevitably to debate. It was by no means clear to fans of Collins' novels that she was the ideal Katniss Everdeen. One fan response, reprinted from a student newspaper in *Huffington Post* and then spread across social media, condemned the choice for removing the racial ambiguity of 'olive-skinned' Katniss in the novels. Eva Schuler was scathing about the casting call's brief for Katniss as 'Caucasian, between ages 15 and 20 . . . "underfed but strong", and "naturally pretty underneath her tomboyishness"' (Schuer 2012). For other fans, she was too old: 21 by the time *Film 1* began shooting, while Katniss was 16. However, reception of her potential as Katniss improved over the coming year. Shooting for *Film 1* began three months before *Silver Linings Playbook* (in July 2011), and both followed the shooting of *X-Men: First Class* in the northern summer of 2010 and premiering around the time *Film 1* went into production. While *Winter's Bone* had been successful, it was neither a blockbuster nor a family- or youth-oriented film, and *Film 1* thus piggybacked on the success of Lawrence's role as Raven/Mystique in the X-Men franchise, with the advantage that the heavy makeup she wore as Mystique allowed more identification between Lawrence and Katniss. Lawrence's blockbuster success drew audiences to her more acclaimed dramatic roles far more than it dignified any artistic claims for the Hunger Games films, although her acting was highly praised. Our point is more broadly that the identification of Katniss with Lawrence was, and continues to be, important to the success of the franchise. We cannot subtract from the Hunger Games either Lawrence's cinematic or extra-cinematic image, including her credibility as a young female actor vocal about additional pressures on young women in the film industry, and representing herself as a feminist.

In October 2015, Lawrence published an essay, 'Why Do I Make Less than my Male Co-Stars?', in the feminist newsletter *Lenny* (co-created by Lena Dunham, creator of HBO's *Girls*). Here, she wrote about trying to have creative input as a young female star:

> I'm over trying to find the 'adorable' way to state my opinion and still be likable! F*ck that. I don't think I've ever worked for a man in charge who spent time contemplating what angle he should use to have his voice heard. It's just heard.
>
> (Lawrence 2015)

Lawrence never distanced herself from popular roles in the wake of her artistic acclaim, and she did not distance this political stance from the Hunger Games either, crediting it to having lived with Katniss for four years:

'I don't see how I couldn't be inspired by this character. I mean I was so inspired by her when I read the books – it's the reason I wanted to play her' (Miller 2015).

In the popular public sphere, as well as in academic scholarship, many feminists see more problems than benefits in such girl-star feminism. Roxane Gay, for example, claims that such voices as Lawrence's may raise awareness 'about what [feminism] means and what the movement aims to achieve', but that a price is paid when it takes 'a pretty young woman' to have 'something to say about feminism' before 'that broad ignorance disappears or is set aside because, at last, we have a more tolerable voice proclaiming the very messages feminism has been trying to impart' (Gay 2014). The Hunger Games has thus become entangled not only with relations between screen girlhood and feminist theory but with debates about celebrity feminism, for which several key voices have been actresses known for girl hero roles, including Emma Watson, who played Hermione in Harry Potter; Kristen Stewart, who played Bella in Twilight; and Maisie Williams, who plays Arya in HBO's *Game of Thrones*.

This vein of celebrity feminism has sometimes undermined oppositions between elevated modes of political or artistic discourse and popular culture, as well as critiquing categorical definitions of feminism (see Taylor 2016). Asked about her most recent film at the time of writing, the art production *Mother* (Aronofsky 2017), Lawrence said:

> 'To me, this is incredibly feminist in the way that these Victorian, patriarchal novels show these loving, amazing husbands that are very slowly and delicately taking away their wives' dignity' . . . Lawrence . . . was reading 'Jane Eyre' during the shoot. 'To be a feminist movie, we don't have to all be women and all be aggressive. Before we knew what feminism was, people were writing these novels that showed women's strength being drained from them'
>
> (quoted in Setoodeh 2017)

With this context in mind, the ease with which feminism becomes a test to be failed in the analysis of girl characters like Katniss is continuous with the dismissal of feminism when the speaker fails an implicit test of ideal feminist subjectivity.

Lawrence's commentary on how she, and other girls and women, might relate to the highly manicured self-images which are her professional stock in trade are also relevant here. It comprises another image of Lawrence, circulating whether she is being dismissed or praised – which is not to deny, reversing Gay's point earlier, that some price is paid when hostile dismissal of feminist voices is a form of feminist credentialing. In response to praise for her understated version of glamour, Lawrence argued the film industry should seek

> a new normal-body type . . . Everybody says, 'We love that there is somebody with a normal body!' And I'm like, 'I don't feel like I have a normal body.' I do Pilates every day. I eat, but I work out a lot more than a normal person. I think we've gotten so used to underweight that when you are a normal weight it's like, 'Oh, my God, she's curvy.' Which is crazy. The bare minimum, just for me, would be to up the ante.
>
> (quoted in Brown 2016)

Our point is not to hold Lawrence up as any resolution of anxious 'post-feminist' discourse, or to deny that feminism can be commodified, although whether that undermines its capacity to do any feminist work is another question. Earlier in 2017, Lawrence was photographed in a US$710 t-shirt by Dior, for which she is 'brand icon', bearing the slogan 'we should all be feminists'. This featured on the cover of *Harper's Bazaar* and spawned a 'trend alert' column on *The Fashion Spot* website, titled 'We Should All Be Wearing Feminist Tees' (Tai 2017). Predictably, this inspired both social media scorn and columns on how to find more affordable versions.

Lawrence's acclaim as an actor is no more important to the Hunger Games franchise, considered as a whole, than her place as a feminist commentator, including her insistence that her feminism is not disallowed by her evident cultural advantages. This relates directly to the characterisation of Katniss which, while it may be dismissed as trivially girly by writers like Stephen King (see introduction), offers images of leadership and courage. The importance of feminist change is equaled by the importance of acknowledging feminist change. The prevalence of popular girl heroes (even while they still work as a surprise), and the viability of a celebrity prepared to be outspoken about ongoing gender inequalities, both belong to an important historical trajectory in which youth film not only has something to say but offers a litmus test.

Katniss does not offer any solution to the structural inequities of Panem. But, in Guy Debord's terms, Katniss creates a series of *situations* that expose the intolerable stratification and authoritarianism of Panem – including the berries, Rue's grave, and most of all killing Coin – and she facilitates others. She helps, we could argue, make a new map of Panem, which brings us back to the media work as 'affective map'. For Shaviro, these are maps of how it feels to live in the world, but maps in this sense can be interpreted, used, and *mean* in many ways. Shaviro credits his conception of 'map' to Gilles Deleuze and Felix Guattari, who claim that 'What distinguishes the map from the tracing is that it is entirely oriented toward an experimentation in contact with the real' (1987: 12). The media work as affective map is, then, a speculation – like Snow's troublesome 'hope' and Jameson's or Dyer's 'utopia'. The situations Katniss helps create refer to a reality beyond them that also encompasses Lawrence's dissatisfaction and uncertainties.

At the end of the Hunger Games, riddled with uncertainty about the future their children will face, Katniss embraces Peeta's suggestion that at least they can help them 'understand' the world 'in a way that will make them braver' (*Book 3*: 456). Speculative fiction can create situations in this sense because, like all fantasies, it is simultaneously impossible and socially determined – real and unreal. For contemporary readers Katniss is, at least in part, an assemblage of fantasies about girlhood, and one in which feminism plays an integral role. The Hunger Games, like speculation in general, is not instructive but aspirational. Katniss raises the possibility, including for fans like Lawrence herself, of refusing the authority and coherence of spectacle – of refusing the idea that, to turn a fannish phrase, *resistance is futile*. To quote President Snow: 'If a girl from District Twelve of all places can defy the capitol and walk away unharmed, what is to stop them from doing the same?' (*Book 2*: 25)

Notes

1 For a summary of major movements in conceptualising fandom up to the time the Hunger Games franchise began, see the introduction to Gray, Sandvoss, and Harrington (2007).
2 The exhibition closed in September 2017 and is not scheduled anywhere else at the time of writing, but that month Lionsgate announced plans for 'Lionsgate Entertainment City' in Times Square, New York City, which would include a Hunger Games-themed flight simulator.
3 As in all large fandoms more marginal conversations form around 'rare pairings', such as 'Clato' fans interested in Cato/Clove (see www.quora.com/What-was-Cato-and-Cloves-relationship-like) or alternative points of narrative focus, such as Finnick or Snow's granddaughter.
4 The. pn code is actually the country extension for Pitcairn Islands.

Bibliography

Adorno, T. and M. Horkheimer. (2002) *Dialectic of Enlightenment: Philosophical Fragments* (orig. 1944), Stanford, CA: Stanford University Press.

Althusser, L. (2006) 'Ideology and Ideological State Apparatuses (Notes Towards an Investigation)' (orig. 1970), in Sharma, A. and A. Gupta (eds) *The Anthropology of the State: A Reader*, Oxford: Blackwell, pp. 86–111.

Altman, R. (1984) 'A Semantic/Syntactic Approach to Film Genre', *Cinema Journal*, 23:3, pp. 6–18.

Ariès, P. (1962) *Centuries of Childhood: A Social History of Family Life*, New York: Vintage Books.

Attebery, B. (2004) 'Fantasy as Mode, Genre, Formula', in Sandner, D. (ed) *Fantastic Literature: A Critical Reader*, Westport: Greenwood Publishing Group, pp. 293–309.

Barrie, J. M. (1911) *Peter and Wendy*, New York: C. Scribner's Sons.

Barthes, R. (1977) 'The Death of the Author', in *Image, Music, Text*, London: Fontana, pp. 142–148.

Basu, B. (2013) 'What Faction Are You In? The Pleasure of Being Sorted in Veronica Roth's Divergent', in Hintz, C., B. Basu and K. R. Broad (eds) *Contemporary Dystopian Fiction for Young Adults: Brave New Teenagers*, London: Routledge, pp. 19–34.

Beck, U. (1992) *Risk Society: Towards a New Modernity*, London: Sage.

Belton, J. (2014) 'If Film Is Dead, What Is Cinema?', *Screen*, 55: 4, pp. 460–470.

Benton, M., M. Dolan, and R. Zisch (1997) 'Teen Films: An Annotated Bibliography', *Journal of Popular Film and Television*, 25:2, pp. 83–88.

Bordwell, D. (2013) *Narration in the Fiction Film*, London: Routledge.

Bourdaa, M. (2016) 'I Am Not a Tribute: The Transmedia Strategy of *The Hunger Games* vs Fan Activism', in Derhy Kurtz, B. W. L. and M. Bourdaa (eds) *The Rise of Transtexts: Challenges and Opportunities*, Oxford: Routledge, pp. 90–103.

Bourdieu, P. (1977) *Outline of a Theory of Practice* (orig. 1972), Cambridge: Cambridge University Press.

Bourdieu, P. (2002) 'The Forms of Capital' (orig. 1986), in Biggart, N. W. (ed) *Readings in Economic Sociology*, Oxford: Blackwell, pp. 280–307.

Brown, J. and N. St. Clair (2002) *Declarations of Independence: Empowered Girls in Young Adult Literature, 1990–2001*, Lanham, MD: Scarecrow Press.

Brown, L. (2016) 'Jennifer Lawrence: Truth and Beauty', *Harpers Bazaar*, 7 April, www.harpersbazaar.com/culture/features/a14989/jennifer-lawrence-interview-news/.

Brown, W. (2015) *Undoing the Demos: Neoliberalism's Stealth Revolution*, Cambridge, MA: MIT Press.

Burnett, F. H. (1911) *The Secret Garden*, New York: F A Stokes.

Butler, J. (1993) *Bodies That Matter: On the Discursive Limits of Sex*, New York: Routledge.

Butler, J. (2000) 'The Force of Fantasy: Feminism, Mapplethorpe, and Discursive Excess' (orig. 1990), in Cornell, D. (ed) *Feminism and Pornography*, Oxford: Oxford University Press, pp. 487–508.

Campbell, J. (1949) *The Hero With a Thousand Faces*, New York: Pantheon Books.

Carles, P. and P. Bourdieu (2001) *La Sociologie est un Sport de Combat*, France: CP Productions: VF Films Productions.

Carroll, L. (2002) *Alice's Adventures in Wonderland* and *Through the Looking-Glass* (orig. 1869 and 1871), Florence: Giunti Editore, S.P.A.

Claeys, G. and L. T. Sargent (eds) (1999a) *The Utopia Reader*, New York: New York University Press.

Claeys, G. and L. T. Sargent (1999b) 'Introduction', in Claeys, G. and L. T. Sargent (eds) *The Utopia Reader*, New York: New York University Press, pp. 1–16.

Clover, C. (1992) *Men, Women, and Chainsaws: Gender in the Modern Horror Film*, Princeton: Princeton University Press.

Cole, R., C. Driscoll and L. Grealy (2018) in Grealy, L., C. Driscoll and A. Hickey-Moody (eds) *Youth, Technology, Governance, Experience: Adults Understanding Young People*, London: Routledge.

Collins, S. (2008–2010) *The Hunger Games Trilogy*, New York: Scholastic.

Considine, D. (1985) *The Cinema of Adolescence*, New York: McFarland.

De Beauvoir, S. (1949) *Le Deuxième Sexe*, Paris: Gallimard.

De Lauretis, T. (1984) 'Desire in Narrative', in *Alice Doesn't: Feminism, Semiotics, Cinema*, Bloomington: Indiana University Press.

Debord, G. (1967) 'Society of the Spectacle', *Marxists.org*, www.marxists.org/reference/archive/debord/society.htm.

Deleuze, G. (1990) *The Logic of Sense* (orig. 1969), New York: Columbia University Press.

Deleuze, G. (1993) *The Fold: Leibniz and the Baroque* (orig. 1988), London: Athlone Press.

Deleuze, G. and F. Guattari (1987) *A Thousand Plateaus: Capitalism and Schizophrenia* (orig. 1980), Minneapolis: University of Minnesota Press.

Dobbins, A. (2013) 'Catching Fire: Why I'm Team Gale', *Vulture*, 15 November, www.vulture.com/2013/11/catching-fire-choose-gale-not-peeta.html.

Doherty, T. (2002) *Teenagers and Teenpics: The Juvenilization of American Movies*, *2nd edition*, Philadelphia: Temple University Press.

Dorsey-Elson, L. K. (2013) ' "Twilight Moms" and the "Female Midlife Crisis": Life Transitions, Fantasy, and Fandom', in Bucciferro, C. (ed) *The Twilight Saga: Exploring the Global Phenomenon*, Lanham, MD: Scarecrow Press, pp. 65–78.

Dries, K. (2013) 'Get Your Bougie Capitol Self Some Hunger Games Makeup', *Jezebel*, 14 August, https://jezebel.com/get-your-bougie-capitol-self-some-hunger-games-makeup-1137445487.

Driscoll, C. (1997) 'The Little Girl', *AntiTHESIS*, 8:2, pp. 79–100.

Driscoll, C. (2002) *Girls: Feminine Adolescence in Popular Culture and Cultural Theory*, New York: Columbia University Press.

Driscoll, C. (2009) *Modernist Cultural Studies*, Gainesville: University Press of Florida.

Driscoll, C. (2011) *Teen Film: A Critical Introduction*, London: Bloomsbury Publishing.

Driscoll, C. (2013) 'The Mystique of the Young Girl', *Feminist Theory*, 14:3, pp. 285–294.

Driscoll, C. and A. Heatwole (2016) 'Glass and Game: The Speculative Girl Hero', in Gelder, K. (ed) *The Palgrave Handbook of Popular Fiction*, New York: Palgrave Macmillan, pp. 261–283.

Dyer, R. (1992) *Only Entertainment*, New York: Routledge.

Dyhouse, C. (1981) *Girls Growing Up in Late Victorian and Edwardian England*, London: Routledge and Kegan Paul.

Early, F. H. and K. Kennedy (2003) *Athena's Daughters: Television's New Women Warriors*, New York: Syracuse University Press.

Eisenhauer, J. (2004) 'Mythic Figures and Lived Identities: Locating the "Girl" in Feminist Discourse', in Harris, A. (ed) *All About the Girl: Culture, Power and Identity*, New York: Routledge, pp. 79–90.

Entertainment Software Association (2017) *Essential Facts About the Computer and Video Game Industry 2017*, www.theesa.com/wp-content/uploads/2017/04/EF2017_FinalDigital.pdf.

Erikson, E. (1968) *Identity, Youth and Crisis*, New York: W. W. Norton Co.

Faulkner, J. (2011) *The Importance of Being Innocent: Why We Worry About Children*, Melbourne: Cambridge University Press.

Ferris, S. and M. Young (eds) (2008) *Chick Flicks: Contemporary Women at the Movies*, New York: Routledge.

Foucault, M. (1977) *Discipline and Punish* (orig. 1975), London: Penguin.

Foucault, M. (1978) *The History of Sexuality, Vol. 1: An Introduction* (orig. 1976), New York: Random House.

Foucault, M. (1997) *Society Must Be Defended: Lectures at the Collège de France, 1975–1976*, New York: St. Martin's Press.

French, E. (2006) *Selling Shakespeare to Hollywood: The Marketing of Filmed Shakespeare Adaptations From 1989 Into the New Millennium*, Hatfield: University of Hertfordshire Press.

Friedan, B. (2001) *The Feminine Mystique* (orig. 1963), New York: W. W. Norton.

Frow, J. (2014) *Genre: The New Critical Idiom, 2nd editions*, New York: Routledge.

Frye, N. (2004) 'The Mythos of Summer: Romance' (orig. 1957), in Sandner, D. (ed) *Fantastic Literature: A Critical Reader*, Westport: Greenwood Publishing, pp. 108–116.

Gatens, M. (2003) 'Power, Bodies, and Difference', in Cahill, A. J. and J. Hansen (eds) *Continental Feminism Reader*, Lanham: Rowman and Littlefield, pp. 258–275.

Gay, R. (2014) 'Emma Watson? Jennifer Lawrence? These Aren't the Feminists You're Looking For', *The Guardian*, 10 October, www.theguardian.com/commentisfree/2014/oct/10/-sp-jennifer-lawrence-emma-watson-feminists-celebrity.

Gennep, van, A. (1909) *Les Rites de Passage*, Paris: Nourry.

Gill, R. (2007) 'Postfeminist Media Culture: Elements of a Sensibility', *European Journal of Cultural Studies*, 10:2, pp. 147–166.

Glaubman, J. (2018) *'Deplorable Cultus': Populism, Globalization, and* The Lord of the Rings, Cornell University, USA, PhD dissertation.

Gordon, C. (1991) 'Governmental Rationality: An Introduction', in Burchell, G., C. Gordon and P. Miller (eds) *The Foucault Effect: Studies in Governmentality*, Chicago: Chicago University Press, pp. 1–51.

Graser, M. (2013) 'Suzanne Collins Breaks Silence to Support "The Hunger Games: Catching Fire"', *Variety*, 29 October, http://variety.com/2013/film/news/suzanne-collins-breaks-silence-to-support-the-hunger-games-catching-fire-1200775202/.

Grealy, L. (2018) 'Common Sense in the Government of Youth and Sex', in Grealy, L., C. Driscoll and A. Hickey-Moody (eds) *Youth, Technology, Government, Experience: Adults Understanding Young People*, London: Routledge.

Guanio-Uluru, L. (2016) 'Female Focalizers and Masculine Ideals: Gender as Performance in Twilight and the Hunger Games', *Children's Literature in Education*, 47:3, pp. 209–224.

Hains, R. (2014) *The Princess Problem: Guiding Our Girls Through the Princess-Obsessed Years*, Chicago: Sourcebooks, Inc.

Harris, A. (2004a) *Future Girl: Young Women in the Twenty-First Century*, New York: Routledge.

Harris, A. (2004b) 'Jamming Girl Culture: Young Women and Consumer Citizenship', in Harris, A. (ed) *All About the Girl: Culture, Power, and Identity*, New York: Routledge, pp. 163–172.

The Harry Potter Alliance (2015) 'What We Do' and 'Success Stories: Odds in Our Favour', www.thehpalliance.org/.

Heatwole, A. (2016) 'Disney Girlhood: Princess Generations and Once Upon a Time', *Studies in the Humanities*, 43:1, pp. 1–19.

Helford, E. R. (2000) 'Introduction', in Helford, E. R. (ed) *Fantasy Girls: Gender in the New Universe of Science Fiction and Fantasy Television*, Lanham: Rowman and Littlefield, pp. 1–12.

Henry, A. (2004) *Not My Mother's Sister: Generational Conflict and Third-Wave Feminism*, Bloomington: Indiana University Press.

Hills, E. (1999) 'From "Figurative Males" to Action Heroines: Further Thoughts on Active Women in the Cinema', *Screen*, 40:1, pp. 38–50.

Hills, M. (2002) *Fan Cultures*, London: Routledge.

Hills, M. (2003) 'Star Wars in Fandom, Film Theory, and the Museum', in Stringer, J. (ed) *Movie Blockbusters*, New York: Routledge, pp. 178–189.

Horne, J. C. (2012) 'Fantasy, Subjectivity, and Desire in Twilight and Its Sequels', in Morey, A. (ed) *Genre, Reception and Adaptation in the Twilight Series*, Farnham: Ashgate, pp. 29–46.

Jameson, F. (1975) 'Magical Narratives: Romance as Genre', *New Literary History*, 7:1, pp. 135–163.

Jameson, F. (1981) *The Political Unconscious: Narrative as a Socially Symbolic Act*, New York: Cornell University Press.

Jameson, F. (1982) 'Progress Versus Utopia; or, Can We Imagine the Future?', *Science Fiction Studies*, 9:2, www.depauw.edu/sfs/backissues/27/jameson.html.

Jameson, F. (2004) 'The Politics of Utopia', *New Left Review*, 25, pp. 35–54.

Jancovich, M. (1996) *Rational Fears: American Horror in the 1950s*, Manchester: Manchester University Press.

Jenkins, H. (2006) *Convergence Culture: Where Old and New Media Collide*, New York: New York University Press.

Jensen, J. (1992) 'Fandom as Pathology: The Consequences of Characterization', in Lewis, L. A. (ed) *The Adoring Audience: Fan Culture and Popular Media*, Hove: Psychology Press, pp. 9–29.

Johnson, D. (2007) 'Factions, Institutions, and Constitutive Hegemonies of Fandom', in Gray, J., C. Sandvoss and C. L. Harrington (eds) *Fandom: Identities and Communities in a Mediated World*, New York: New York University Press, pp. 369–386.

Johnston, K. M. (2011) *Science Fiction Film: A Critical Introduction*, London: Berg.

Kinder, M. (1991) *Playing With Power in Movies, Television, and Video Games: From Muppet Babies to Teenage Mutant Ninja Turtles*, Oakland, CA: University of California Press.

King, G. (2003) 'Spectacle, Narrative, and Spectacular Hollywood Blockbuster', in Stringer, J. (ed) *Movie Blockbusters*, New York: Routledge, pp. 114–127.

King, S. (2008) 'The Hunger Games', *Entertainment Weekly*, 8 September, http://ew.com/article/2008/09/08/hunger-games.

Klock, G. (2002) *How to Read Superhero Comics and Why*, New York: Continuum.

Kornfield, S. (2016) 'The Hunger Games: Understanding Postfeminist and Postracial Ideologies', *Teaching Media Quarterly*, 4:4, pp. 1–9.

Lawrence, F. (Director) (2015). *The Hunger Games: Mockingjay—Part 2* [Film]. USA: Lionsgate. November 19, 2015. Film.

Lawrence, F. (Director). (2013). *The Hunger Games: Catching Fire* [Film]. USA: Lionsgate. November 11, 2013. Film.

Lawrence, F. & Ross, G. (Director) (2014). *The Hunger Games: Mockingjay—Part 1* [Film]. USA: Lionsgate. November 19, 2014. Film.

Lawrence, J. (2015) 'Jennifer Lawrence: "Why Do I Make Less Than My Male Co-Stars?"', *Lenny*, 14 October, www.lennyletter.com/work/a147/jennifer-lawrence-why-do-i-make-less-than-my-male-costars/.

Le Guin, U. K. (1979) 'From Elfland to Poughkeepsie', in *The Language of the Night: Essays on Fantasy and Science Fiction*, New York: Ultramarine Publishing.

Lionsgate. (2017). *The Hunger Games Exhibition*. Retrieved from http://www.thehungergamesexhibition.com/.

Mallan, K. and S. Pearce (2003) *Youth Cultures: Texts, Images, and Identities*, London: Praeger.

Margolis, R. (2008) 'A Killer Story: An Interview With Suzanne Collins, Author of "The Hunger Games"', *School Library Journal*, online, 1 September, www.slj. com/2008/09/interviews/under-cover/a-killer-story-an-interview-with-suzanne-collins-author-of-the-hunger-games/.

Marx, K. (1976) *Capital, Vol. 1* (orig. 1867), New York: Modern Library.

McRobbie, A. (2009) *The Aftermath of Feminism: Gender, Culture and Social Change*, London: Sage.

Mead, M. (1928) *Coming of Age in Samoa*, New York: William Morrow & Co.

Meyer, S. (2005–2008) *Twilight Series*, New York: Little, Brown and Company.

Miller, J. (2012) '"She Has No Idea, the Effect She Can Have": Katniss and the Politics of Gender', in Dunn, G., N. Michaud and W. Irwin (eds) *The Hunger Games and Philosophy: A Critique of Pure Treason*, Hoboken, NJ: John Wiley and Sons, pp. 145–161.

Miller, J. (2015) 'Jennifer Lawrence Is Just as Inspired by *Hunger Games* Heroine Katniss Everdeen as You Are', *Vanity Fair's HWD*, 3 November, www.vanityfair. com/hollywood/2015/11/jennifer-lawrence-hunger-games-katniss-everdeen.

Moylan, T. (1998) 'Introduction: Jameson and Utopia', *Utopian Studies*, 9:2, pp. 1–7.

Mueller, H. (2017) *States of Fandom: Community, Constituency, Public Sphere*, Cornell University, unpublished PhD dissertation, http://doi.org/10.7298/X4SQ8XD7.

Mulvey, L. (1975) 'Visual Pleasure and Narrative Cinema', *Screen*, 16:3, pp. 6–18.

Murray, S. and L. Ouellette (eds) (2004) *Reality TV: Remaking Television Culture*, New York: NYU Press.

Nelson, C. and L. Vallone (1994) *The Girl's Own: Cultural Histories of the Anglo-American Girl, 1830–1915*, Athens: University of Georgia.

O'Connor, C. J. (2010) *The Cultural Significance of the Child Star*, New York: Routledge.

Pipher, M. (1994) *Reviving Ophelia: Saving the Selves of Adolescent Girls*, New York: Putnam.

Polo, S. (2012) 'The Best of CafePress' New Official Hunger Games Merchandise Store', *The Mary Sue*, online, 23 February, www.themarysue.com/official-hunger-games-merchandise/.

Propp, V. (1968) *Morphology of the Folktale*, Bloomington: American Folklore Society.

Radway, J. (1984) *Reading the Romance: Women, Patriarchy, and Popular Culture*, Chapel Hill: University of North Carolina Press.

Rich, A. (1980), 'Compulsory Heterosexuality and Lesbian Existence', *Signs*, 5:4, pp. 631–660.

Riggan, W. (1981). *Pícaros, Madmen, Naïfs, and Clowns: The Unreliable First-person Narrator*. Univ. of Oklahoma Press: Norman.

Riviere, J. (1929) 'Womanliness as a Masquerade', *International Journal of Psycho-Analysis*, 9, pp. 303–313.

Ross, G. (Director) (2012). *The Hunger Games* [Film]. USA: Lionsgate.

Rousseau, J. J. (1979) *Emile, or On Education* (orig. 1762), New York: Basic Books.

Schubart, R. (2007) *Super Bitches and Action Babes: The Female Hero in Popular Cinema, 1970–2006*, Jefferson, NC: McFarland and Co. Ltd.

Schuer, H. E. L. (2012) '"Hunger Games" Casting: Why Jennifer Lawrence Shouldn't Play Katniss', *Huffington Post*, 2 March, www.huffingtonpost.com.au/entry/hunger-games-movie_n_1314053.

Setoodeh, R. (2017) 'Jennifer Lawrence on Why "Mother!" Is a Feminist Movie', *Variety*, 12 September, http://variety.com/2017/film/news/jennifer-lawrence-on-why-mother-is-a-feminist-movie-1202555294/.

Shary, T. (2014) *Generation Multiplex: The Image of Youth in American Cinema Since 1980, 2nd edition*, Austin, TX: University of Texas Press.

Shary, T. and A. Seibel (eds) (2007) *Youth Culture and Global Cinema*, Austin: University of Texas Press.

Shaviro, S. (2010) *Post Cinematic Affect*, Blue Ridge Summit, PA: John Hunt Publishing.

Shaviro, S. (2011) 'What Is the Post Cinematic?', *The Pinocchio Theory*, 11 August, www.shaviro.com/Blog/?p=992.

Silver, A. (2010) 'Twilight Is Not Good for Maidens: Gender, Sexuality, and the Family in Stephenie Meyer's Twilight Series', *Studies in the Novel*, 42:1–2, pp. 121–138.

'Situationist Manifesto' (1960) *Internationale Situationniste*, #4, June 1960, www.cddc.vt.edu/sionline/si/manifesto.html.

Skeggs, B. (2004) 'Introduction', in Adkins, L. and B. Skeggs (eds) *Feminism After Bourdieu*, Oxford: Blackwell, pp. 19–34.

Skeggs, B. and H. Wood (2011) *Reality Television and Class*, New York: Palgrave Macmillan.

Smith, L. (1993) '"Take Back Your Mink": Lewis Carroll, Child Masquerade and the Age of Consent', *Art History*, 16:3, pp. 369–385.

Stedman, A. (2013) 'Stephen King Calls Twilight "Tweenager Porn," Talks "The Shining" Sequel', *Variety*, 23 September, http://variety.com/2013/film/news/stephen-king-calls-twilight-tweenager-porn-talks-the-shining-sequel-1200662812/.

Tai, C. (2017) 'Trend Alert: We Should All Be Wearing Feminist Tees', *The Fashion Spot*, 6 January, www.thefashionspot.com/style-trends/732319-feminist-t-shirts-apparel/#VspRElM2lYjar58D.99.

Tasker, Y. (1993) *Spectacular Bodies: Gender, Genre and the Action Cinema*, London: Routledge.

Taylor, A. (2012) '"The Urge Towards Love Is an Urge Towards (Un)Death": Romance, Masochistic Desire and Postfeminism and the Twilight Novels', *International Journal of Cultural Studies*, 15:1, pp. 31–46.

Taylor, A. (2016) *Celebrity and the Feminist Blockbuster*, New York: Palgrave Macmillan.

Taylor, J. (2014) 'Romance and the Female Gaze Obscuring Gendered Violence in the Twilight Saga', *Feminist Media Studies*, 14:3, pp. 388–402.

Tiqqun (2012) *Preliminary Materials for a Theory of the Young-girl* (orig. 1999), Cambridge, MA: MIT Press.

Todorov, T. (2000) 'Definition of the Fantastic' (orig. 1970), in Gelder, K. (ed) *The Horror Reader*, London: Routledge, pp. 14–19.

Tolkien, J. R. R. (1954) *The Fellowship of the Ring*, London: Allen and Unwin.

Turner, V. (1969) *The Ritual Process: Structure and Anti-Structure*, London: Routledge & Kegan Paul.

Walters, J. (2011) *Fantasy Film: A Critical Introduction*, London: Berg.

Wezner, K. (2012) ' "Perhaps I Am Watching You Now": Panem's Panopticons', in Pharr, M. F. and L. A. Clark (eds) *Of Bread, Blood and the Hunger Games: Critical Essays on the Suzanne Collins Trilogy*, Jefferson, NC: McFarland and Company, Inc., pp. 148–157.

Woloshyn, V., N. Taber, and L. Lane (2013) 'Discourses of Masculinity and Femininity in *The Hunger Games: "Scarred," "Bloody," and "Stunning"* ', *International Journal of Social Science Studies*, 1:1, pp. 150–160.

Woolf, V. (1945) *A Room of One's Own* (orig. 1929), London: Harmondsworth.

Zipes, J. (1997) *Happily Ever After: Fairy Tales, Children, and the Culture Industry*, New York: Routledge.

Index

Note: Italicized page numbers indicate a figure on the corresponding page.

action genre 6, 85
action movie conventions 44–50, *45*
Adorno, Theodor 7, 85
affective map 87
Alice (*Wonderland* character)
    37–39
Alice's Adventures in Wonderland
    (Carroll) 37, 38–39
Alma Coin (character) 11, 27, 39, 40,
    74, 77
Althusser, Louis 75–76
Altman, Rick 86
Annie (character) 27, 55
Ariès, Phillipe 25, 35–36

Bakhtin, Maikhail 4
Banks, Elizabeth 12
Barthes, Roland 6
becoming, defined 27, 35, 49
becoming-woman 47
Bella Cullen (*Twilight* character)
    64–67
Belton, John 86
Bentley, Wes 12–13
bildungsroman 16
Bourdieu, Pierre 80–84
Brave (film) 20
Brave New World (Huxley) 75
bridal promise 51–56
Brown, Wendy 14–15
Buffy the Vampire Slayer franchise 8,
    46, 48
Burton, Tim 39
Butler, Judith 59, 63

Caesar Flickerman (character) 13
Campbell, Joseph 20–21
can-do girls 15
capitalist commodity culture 6, 13,
    74–77, 81–84
Capitol Couture magazine 91
Capitol.pn site 91–93
Carroll, Lewis 37–38
Carter, Lynda 45
celebrity feminism 96–97
celebrity subgenre 29
chick flicks 56
Cinderella (film) 20
cinematic gaze 3
Cinna (character) 12, 32, 33–34, 48, 59, 61
Claflin, Sam 10
Clover, Carol 46–47
Collins, Suzanne: as co-producer 90;
    fanbase of 88; introduction to 1–2,
    4; merchandising debate 93; story
    inspiration 13–14, 25
colonialism 35
combat sequences 45
commodity fetishism 7
commodity society 7
Communist Manifesto 76
Considine, David 41
Coriolanus Snow (character) 4, 27,
    39–40, 56
Cressida (character) 42
cult blockbuster 90

Debord, Guy 7, 76, 97
de Lauretis, Teresa 22

Deleuze, Gilles 27, 47, 49
depersonalising media effects 31
'Desire in Narrative' (de Lauretis) 22
disciplinary power 69, 71
Disney, Walt 38
Divergent franchise 8, 28
docusoap subgenre 29
'double entanglement' of postfeminist
   discourse 59
Dyer, Richard 79–80, 98
dystopian tenor of *Hunger Games*:
   capitalist commodity culture 6,
   13, 74–77, 81–84; introduction to
   68; politics of 74–80; surveillance
   images 69–74, *72, 73*

Early, Frances 57
educated class 81, 82
Edward Cullen (*Twilight* character)
   64–67
Effie Trinket (character) 12
Ellen Ripley (*Aliens* character) 46–47
Engels, Friedrich 76
entertainment experience 79–80
Erikson, Erik 24
expansion of consciousness 21

fan activism 92
fan culture 88–94, *89*
fan paraphernalia 89
fantasy genre of *Hunger Games*:
   attraction of 19–23; introduction
   to 19; reality games 28–34, *30, 32*;
   tributes in 10, 23–28
fascist state 77
Faulkner, Joanne 25
feminised plot-space 22
feminist hero 51, 63
feminist theory 96–97
figurative males 46
Finnick Odair (character) 10, 34,
   55–56, 59
first-person narration 2–3, 41
Foucault, Michel 14, 69, 72
franchising girlhood 2–8, *5*
Freud, Sigmund 22, 24
Friedan, Betty 8
Frow, John 6
Frozen (film) 20
Frye, Northrop 63

Gale Hawthorne (character) 10,
   53–54, 65
gamedoc subgenre 29
Gatens, Moira 61
Gay, Roxane 96
gender codes 16
gender identity 33
generic expectations of specialness 30
genre films 6
Gill, Rosalind 61
girl-centric maternalism of feminism 48
girl culture 20, 32
girl hero 1, 35–40, *40*; *see also* Katniss
   Everdeen; speculative girl hero
'girl power' feminism 15
governmentality 14
Greasy Sae (character) 11
Grossman, Lev 29
Guattari, Felix 27, 97

haecceity 27
Halloween (film) 46
Hamilton, Linda 46
Harrelson, Woody 11
Harris, Anita 15, 28, 58
Harry Potter Alliance's campaign 92
Harry Potter franchise 8, 23–24, 28,
   88, 91
Haymitch Abernathy (character) 11, 12,
   30–31, 34, 39, 48–49, 53
hegemonic gender codes 16
Helford, Elyce 45–46, 57
heroic quest 20, 21
heroic romance formula 22
The Hero With a Thousand Faces
   (Campbell) 21
heteronormative romance 53
Hills, Elizabeth 46, 48, 88, 91
The History of Sexuality (Foucault) 14
Hoffman, Phillip Seymour 12
Horkheimer, Max 7, 85
Horne, Jackie C. 66
horror genre 6, 87
The Hunger Games (film): climactic
   moment of 76; early dramatic
   sequences of 25–26; heroic trial
   in 23; introduction to 1; Katniss's
   greatest weakness 31; Katniss's
   songs 78; makeover scenes 32;
   mechanism of surveillance 70–71;

Panem's failure 11–12; Reaping in 26; tributes in 10, 24–25

The Hunger Games: Catching Fire (film): heroic trial in 23; introduction to 1; Katniss's songs 78; mechanism of surveillance 70–71, *72*; references to sex 52, 54; Snow's granddaughter 40; tributes in 10

The Hunger Games: Mockingjay Part 1 (film): introduction to 1; Katniss-Peeta separation 43; literal undergrounds of 23; makeover scenes 32; mechanism of surveillance 73, *73*; references to sex 52; Snow's granddaughter 40

The Hunger Games: Mockingjay Part 2 (film): introduction to 1; Katniss-Peeta separation 43; Katniss's songs 79; literal undergrounds of 23; mechanism of surveillance 73, *73*

Hunger Games Fandom Wiki 89

Hunger Games films: action movie conventions 44–50, *45*; franchising girlhood 2–8, *5*; introduction to 1–2; reality TV in 28–34, *30*, *32*, 83; speculative adolescence 8–13, *11*; teen film conventions 6, 41–44; *Twilight* comparison 64–67; youth at risk 13–18

Hunger Games memes: fan culture 88–94, *89*; introduction to 85; Lawrence, Jennifer 94–98; rebels with a cause 86–88

Hutcherson, Josh 4

iconic imagery 22
iconography 4
identity: debates over 36; gender identity 33; self-evaluation of 38; subcultural identities 41; in teen films 41–44; transformations of 43
ideological state apparatus (ISA) 75–76
independence 36
intertextuality theory 4–6

Jackson, Peter 9
Jameson, Frederic 63, 75, 76, 80, 86, 98
Jenkins, Henry 5–6, 85
Jenkins, Patty 9
Johanna Mason (character) 10

Katniss Barbie dolls 4, *5*
Katniss Everdeen (character): antagonist to 12; charisma of authenticity 34; evaluation of choices 16–17; franchising girlhood 2–8, *5*; greatest weakness 31; heroic quest of 20; identity transformations 43; introduction to 2, 35; Mockingjay transformation 23, 29, 50, 59, 73–74, 77; modern girlhood emergence 35–40, *40*; reality TV transformation of 31–32, *32*; sexualised love interests 10; speculative girl hero 8–9, 39, 46, 57–64, *62*; survival of 28–29; teen films and 41–44; wedding dress design 33–34
kidult fiction 36
Kinder, Marsha 4–5
King, Stephen 17
Kravitz, Lenny 12

Lawrence, Jennifer 3, 4, 55, 94–98
Le Guin, Ursula K. 23
Lenny letter 95
Lewis, C.S. 29
lex insita principle 81
liminality 25
Lionsgate films 85, 91, 93
The Lord of the Rings (Tolkien) 24
Lotman, Jurij 22
Lucas, George 8

Magical Narratives 76
Magicians novels 29
Mags (character) 27
makeover subgenre 29, 32
Maleficent (film) 20
Mallan, Kerry 27
Malone, Jena 10
manga 8
Marx, Karl 7, 76
Marxist theory 6, 74
The Mary Sue 93–94
mass culture 7
maturity considerations 36
McRobbie, Angela 57, 58–59, 63, 66
Mead, Margaret 24
merchandising 6, 90–91
merchant class 81
military force 70

Miller, Jessica 58
Mockingjay transformation 23, 29, 50, 59, 73–74, 77
Moore, Julianne 11
moral compass of the story 3
morality encounters 43
More, Thomas 76
Motion Picture Association of America 44
Mulvey, Laura 8, 21
Murray, Susan 29, 69

Nania novels 29
narrative form 22
Nazism 78
neo(liberal) state 13–18
1984 (Orwell) 72
normative performative 61

Okeniyi, Dayo 27
Orwell, George 71–72
Ouellette, Laurie 29, 69

Panem's failure 11–12
Pearce, Sharyn 27
Peeta Mellark (character) 4, 27, 31, 33, 43, 53–56
philosophy of capture 47
physical danger sequences 45
Plutarch Heavensbee (character) 12–13
political geography 68
politics of *Hunger Games* 74–80
post-adolescence questions 43
Post Cinematic Affect (Shaviro) 86–87
postfeminism 15, 16, 57, 58–64
Prim Everdeen (character) 3, 25–26, 54
Propp, Vladimir 49

Raw Materials for a Theory of the Young-Girl (Tiqqun) 7
ready-made emotional response 23
reality sitcoms subgenre 29
reality TV in *Hunger Games* 28–34, *30*, *32*, 83
Reaping in *Hunger Games* 26, 57
rebels with a cause 86–88
reflexive modernity 17
reproduction of labour 81
Reviving Ophelia (Pipher) 15–16
riot grrrls 15

risk society concept 17
rite of passage stories 24
romance genre 6
Roman gladiator games 13
romantic cycle 21
romantic sub-narrative 35
Roth, Veronica 8
Rousseau, Jean-Jacques 36
Rowling, J.K. 8
Rue (character) 11, 27, 55, 59
Russell, David O. 94

Sailor Moon franchise 8
Sarah Connor (*Terminator* character) 46, 47, 48
science fiction/fantasy genre 6, 87; *see also* fantasy genre of *Hunger Games*
science fiction genre 19–20
'second wave' feminism 16
The Secret Garden (Burnett) 37
self-definition 57
self-destructive 'melancholia' 16
self-imposed inhibition 66
self-representation 38
Seneca Crane (character) 12–13, 70–71
sex in *Hunger Games* 52–53
shared knowledge of fans 89
Shary, Timothy 86
Shaviro, Steven 86–87
Situationists 7
Skeggs, Beverly 61, 84
slogan for The Games 17
Snow's granddaughter (character) 39–40
social anxiety 24
social resistance 87
Society of the Spectacle (Debord) 7
sovereign power 70
sparagmos, defined 21
spectacle in defining society 74–80
speculative adolescence 8–13, *11*
speculative fiction 16, 20, 98
speculative girl hero 8–9, 39, 46, 57–64, *62*
star-crossed lovers 55
Star Wars franchise 8, 45
state-media complex 25
subcultural identities 41
super-heroic action films 9

supreme ordeal 21
surveillance images 69–74,
  72, 73
Sutherland, Donald 11
symbolic power 26

talent contests subgenre 29
teen angst 51–56
teen film conventions 6, 41–44
teen romance plot in *Hunger Games*:
  introduction to 51; speculative girl
  hero 8–9, 39, 46, 57–64, *62*; teen
  angst and bridal promise 51–56, *52*
teen/youth film genre 6
television girl-centered stories 9
The Terminator (film) 46, 47, 48
The Texas Chainsaw Massacre
  (film) 46
Thresh (character) 27
Through the Looking-Glass (Carroll)
  37, 38
Todorov, Tzvetan 20
Tolkien, J.R.R. 9, 24
Transmedia Alice 39
tributes in *Hunger Games* 10,
  23–28
Tucci, Stanley 13
Turner, Victor 24

tween fiction 36
Twilight franchise 23–24, 64–67

unreliable narrator 2
Utopia (More) 76
Utopian longings 76
utopian sensibility 80

van Gennep, Arnold 24
Vindication of the Rights of Woman
  (Wollstonecraft) 36
virginal girl heroes 53
vulnerability 36

war machine 49
Weaver, Sigourney 46
Whedon, Joss 8
Wonder Woman (film) 9, 45
Woolf, Virginia 8

X-Men franchise 95

young adult (YA) heroines 16, 85
YoungGirl 7
youth at risk 13–18
youth cinema 1
youth culture 42
youth-oriented conventions 85

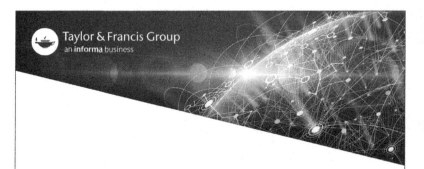

Taylor & Francis Group
an **informa** business

Taylor & Francis eBooks

www.taylorfrancis.com

A single destination for eBooks from Taylor & Francis
with increased functionality and an improved user
experience to meet the needs of our customers.

90,000+ eBooks of award-winning academic content in
Humanities, Social Science, Science, Technology, Engineering,
and Medical written by a global network of editors and authors.

TAYLOR & FRANCIS EBOOKS OFFERS:

A streamlined
experience for
our library
customers

A single point
of discovery
for all of our
eBook content

Improved
search and
discovery of
content at both
book and
chapter level

REQUEST A FREE TRIAL
support@taylorfrancis.com

 Routledge
Taylor & Francis Group

 CRC Press
Taylor & Francis Group

Printed in the United States
by Baker & Taylor Publisher Services